Women in Jamaica:
A Bibliography of Published
and Unpublished Sources

Women in Jamaica:
A Bibliography of Published
and Unpublished Sources

compiled by
Leona Bobb-Semple

**The Press University
of the West Indies**

Cover illustration (and motifs in text): Oil painting from the collection of Dr and Mrs Owen Jefferson reproduced by courtesy of artist David Pottinger, and by courtesy of Dr and Mrs Owen Jefferson

The Press University of the West Indies
1a Aqueduct Flats Mona
Kingston 7   Jamaica   WI

© 1997 by Leona Bobb-Semple
All rights reserved. Published 1997
Printed in the United States of America
ISBN: 978-976-640-033-0

01   00   99   98   97   5   4   3   2   1

CATALOGUING IN PUBLICATION DATA

Bobb-Semple, Leona
    Women in Jamaica : a bibliography of
    published and unpublished sources / compiled
    by Leona Bobb-Semple

    p.   cm.
    ISBN 976-640-033-4
    1. Women–Jamaica–Bibliography
    I. Title.   II. Women in Jamaica.
    Z7964.J3B62   1997   016 dc–20

Set in 11/13 Times Roman
Book and cover design by Dariel Mayer

To

Leah, Asha and Kalima

and to

the University Women's Group

(University of the West Indies)

Contents

Introduction

Purpose

The primary purpose of this bibliography is to establish control over the published and unpublished sources on women in Jamaica. As a general principle I have sought to be inclusive rather than selective.

The search for sources proved how difficult it is for researchers to locate information on women in Jamaica, as a number of titles fall in the category of grey literature: theses, papers presented at conferences, commissioned reports, unpublished surveys—material which is difficult to locate in published listings and is available only in a limited number of copies.

Scope

There is no limitation in scope except that newspaper articles are excluded, as is material published after 1994. Most of the works identified were written after 1970 as the bulk of the research on women in Jamaica really had its genesis with the declaration of International Women's Year in 1975. Prior to that, research seems to have been concentrated on the twin subjects of the family and fertility. This is reflected in the bibliography in the number of titles that sought either comparatively or otherwise to draw conclusions in this area. Some early research also centered on economic conditions but focused specifically on domestic trade as it related to higglering and market vending. Even here the slant in these early studies on economic conditions was not women-centred but was focused mainly on the informal economic sector. Since the mid seventies, the emphasis has shifted to women researching women's involvement in many spheres of historical, social and economic life in Jamaica.

Certain areas yet to be tapped and recorded include women's involvement in science and technology, politics, trade unionism, religion, and biographical studies, which would give insights into women's contribution in various arenas. There is also a need for more empirical research rather than descriptive material based only on secondary sources and opinion. In sum, the bibliography identifies what already exists, and, in so doing, points to areas where material is lacking.

Collection Process
In an attempt to put together as comprehensive a list as possible, catalogues at the University of the West Indies Library (Mona) and the National Library of Jamaica were used as starting points. These catalogues yielded a small number of citations because of the nature of the material, as discussed above. Use was made of the MEDCARIB and WEST INDIANA databases of the University of the West Indies Library. Databases in the following institutions were also searched: ISER Documentation Centre, and the libraries of the Planning Institute of Jamaica and the Urban Development Corporation. Collections housed at the Sistren Theatre Collective and the Bureau of Women's Affairs were also examined. Numerous bibliographies and citations appearing in books, journal articles, conference papers and theses were also looked at in an effort to identify material.

Citations that the compiler did not locate have been included and will be recognized as these may lack full bibliograhic details and location symbols are not provided.

Arrangement
The bibliographic entries are arranged alphabetically within broad subject groups in one numerical sequence. There are three form groups: Bibliographies, Periodicals and Audiovisuals at the end. Each entry has been placed in the group that predominantly treats the subject content of the citation. Due to the interdisciplinary nature of women's studies some entries could have been placed in more than one group but that practice was not followed. Instead descriptors were assigned in order to highlight various themes in the citations.

Style of Entries
Entries are designed to include all personal and corporate authors responsible for the work, followed by titles, publication details where

present, the number of pages and descriptors. Some citations are followed by annotations and most by location symbols.

Descriptors
All entries except periodicals and laws have been assigned descriptors. An attempt has been made to use descriptors that positively reflect women's issues and to this end descriptors were taken mainly from the terms provided in: *A Women's Thesaurus: an Index of Language to Describe and Locate Information by and about Women*, edited by Mary Ellen S. Capek. Some descriptors are keywords from titles; other words in local usage that are not covered by the thesaurus, such as 'higglering', were also used. Every attempt has been made to ensure consistency in usage particularly for terms appearing in the index. However, all terms following the citations have not been indexed—rather, only the broader terms comprise the index.

Annotations
Annotations have been provided for some items, sometimes in an attempt to indicate content, or to provide additional bibliographic information where it was discovered that an item may have been presented at a conference and subsequently published as an article in a journal. No attempt has been made to draw conclusions as to the usefulness or value of the works, as the bibliography's main aim is to identify and establish some control of the literature rather than to prescribe.

Location Symbols
One location symbol has been assigned for all works verified and located in local libraries. The number of items followed by the location symbol (UWIM) attest to the fact that quite a comprehensive collection on women in Jamaica is housed at the University of the West Indies Library (Mona). As this library system was my point of reference that location was given priority, even though some of the material is available in other libraries. In cases where a non-UWIM location has been assigned, the work has been identified in that collection only.

Indexes
The author index lists alphabetically the personal and corporate authors responsible for the output of the cited work. The subject index was derived from the major descriptor terms provided at the end of each cita-

tion. Cross referencing has been applied in many instances to link related material. These indexes are listed in Appendixes 2 and 3.

Creative Writings

As the bibliography does not include creative writings, the hope is that Appendix 1 will highlight some of the published works of the women for whom literary criticism, interviews, biographical data and other references appear in the bibliography. These works are listed in alphabetical sequence.

Addresses of Libraries

The addresses of libraries housing the material are provided in Appendix 4.

Location Symbols

ISER   Institute of Social and Economic Research, University of the West Indies (Mona, Jamaica)

MINAG   Ministry of Agriculture Library, Jamaica

NLJ   National Library of Jamaica

PIOJ   Planning Institute of Jamaica, Documentation Centre.

STC   Sistren Theatre Collective, Jamaica

UDC   Urban Development Corporation Library, Jamaica

UWIB   University of the West Indies (Cave Hill, Barbados), Faculty of Law Library

UWIM   The Library. University of the West Indies (Mona, Jamaica)

WB   Bureau of Women's Affairs, Jamaica

Arts and Literature

This section covers in the main literary criticism on women's writings, the image of women in literature written by both women and men, and women's involvement in the arts and music. The relatively new area of gender discourse has also been included here. It does not include works of fiction, poetry and drama by women, but for ease of reference a listing of works of authors identified in this section has been included in an appendix.

1   Allison, Helen. *Sistren Song: Popular Theatre in Jamaica.* London: War and Want, 1986. 24 p.
      Sistren Theatre Collective/ Theatre (UWIM)

2   Anderson, B., and W. Langley. "Women as Depicted in Popular Music in Jamaica." Paper presented at the 14th Conference of the Caribbean Studies Association held in Barbados, 23–26 May, 1989. 22 p.
      Popular music/ Lyrics/ Image of women/ Stereotypes/ Reggae music/ Music (ISER)

3   Baker, Thelma. "In a Different Voice: Madness and the Female Condition in Contemporary Fiction." Master's thesis, University of the West Indies, 1990. 69 leaves.
      Thesis looks at the treatment of women in the works of four women writers focusing on the experience of madness as it parallels the female search for self-authenticity. *Jane and Louisa* by Erna Brodber is one of the works considered.
      Feminist literary criticism/ Erna Brodber/ *Jane and Louisa*/ Mentally ill in literature/ Authors (UWIM)

4   Barash, Carol. "The Character of Difference: the Creole Woman as Cultural Mediator in Narratives about Jamaica." *Eighteenth-Century Studies.* Vol. 23, no. 4 (1990): 406–25.
     Cultural heritage/ Women in literature (UWIM)

5   Baugh, Edward. "Goodison on the Road to *Heartease.*" *Journal of West Indian Literature.* Vol. 1, no. 1 (1986): 13–21.
     Lorna Goodison/ Poets/ *Heartease* (UWIM)

6   _____. "Lorna Goodison in the Context of Feminist Criticism." *Journal of West Indian Literature.* Vol. 4, no. 1 (1990): 1–13.
     Lorna Goodison/ Poets/ Feminist literary criticism/ Mother in literature (UWIM)

7   Boxer, David. *Edna Manley: Sculptor;* with a Tribute by Rex Nettleford. Kingston: National Gallery of Jamaica and the Edna Manley Foundation, 1990. 204 p.
     Published on the occasion of the Edna Manley Retrospective Exhibition held at the National Gallery in 1990. Includes a chronology and an exhibition record.
     Edna Manley/ Sculptors/ Artists (UWIM)

8   Bryan, Patricia. "Edna Manley: Sculptor in Retrospect." *Jamaica Journal.* Vol. 23, no. 1 (1990): 28–36.
     Edna Manley/ Sculptors/ Artists (UWIM)

9   Campbell, Elaine. "Two West Indian Heroines: Bita Plant and Fola Piggott." *Caribbean Quarterly.* Vol. 29, no. 2 (1983): 22–29.
     Women in literature/ Claude McKay/ *Banana Bottom*/ George Lamming/ *Season of Adventure* (UWIM)

10   Clarke, Carol Rose. "Woman Redefined in the Novels *Jane and Louisa Will Soon Come Home, Wide Sargasso Sea* and *Juletane.*" Master's thesis, University of the West Indies, 1992. 45 leaves.
     Women in literature/ Erna Brodber/ *Jane and Louisa*/ Jean Rhys/ Authors (UWIM)

11   Cobham-Sander, C. Rhonda. "Women in Jamaican literature, 1900–1950." In "The Creative Writer and West Indian Society." PhD thesis, University of St. Andrews, 1981. p. 195–252.
     Women in literature/ Authors (UWIM)

12   _____. "Getting out of Kumbla: *Jane and Louisa Will Soon Come Home* by Erna Brodber." *Race Today Review.* Vol. 14, no. 1 (1981–1982): 33–34.

Erna Brodber/ *Jane and Louisa/* Authors (UWIM)

13   Cooke, Michael G. "The Strains of Apocalypse: Lamming's *Castle* and Brodber's *Jane and Louisa.*" *Journal of West Indian Literature.* Vol. 4, no. 1 (1990): 28–40.

Male development in literature/ Female development in literature/ Erna Brodber/ *Jane and Louisa/* George Lamming/ *In the Castle of My Skin/* Authors (UWIM)

14   Cooper, Carolyn. "Afro-Jamaican Folk Elements in Brodber's *Jane and Louisa Will Soon Come Home.*" In *Out of the Kumbla: Caribbean Women and Literature,* edited by Carol Boyce Davies and Elaine Savory Fido, p. 279–88. New Jersey: Africa World Press, 1990.

Erna Brodber/ *Jane and Louisa/* Folk themes/ African influences/ Authors (UWIM)

15   _____. "That Cunny Jamma Oman: the Female Sensibility in the Poetry of Louise Bennett." *Jamaica Journal.* Vol. 18, no. 4 (1985): 2–9.

Louise Bennett/ Dialect poetry/ Poets

16   _____. "Disarming Women: Sexual Politics in Neville Dawes's *Interim.*" *Journal of West Indian Literature.* Vol. 2, no. 1 (1987): 55–66.

Neville Dawes/ *Interim/* Sexual politics in literature (UWIM)

17   _____. "Noh Lickle Twang: an Introduction to the Poetry of Louise Bennett". *World Literature Written in English.* Vol. 17, no. 1 (1986): 317–27.

Louise Bennett/ Dialect poetry/ Poets (UWIM)

18   _____. *Noises in the Blood: Orality, Gender and the 'Vulgar' Body of Jamaican Popular Culture.* London: Macmillan, 1993. 214 p.

Popular culture/ Reggae music/ Dance hall music/ Sexuality/ Louise Bennett/ Jean Breeze/ Sistren Theatre Collective/ Music/ Poets/ Popular music (UWIM)

19   _____. "Proverb as Metaphor in the Poetry of Louise Bennett." *Jamaica Journal.* Vol. 17, no. 2 (1984): 21–24.
     Louise Bennett/ Poets/ Dialect poetry (UWIM)

20   _____. "Slackness Hiding from Culture: Erotic Play in the Dancehall, Parts 1 and 2." *Jamaica Journal.* Vol. 22, no. 4 (1989–1990): 12–20 and Vol. 23, no. 1 (1990): 44–51.
     Music/ Dance hall music/ Popular culture/ Image of women/ Sexuality/ Lyrics/ Popular music

21   _____. " 'Uu Se Dat Uman Kyan Don?': Representations of the Female Sexuality in the Lyrics of Bob Marley and Shabba Ranks." Paper presented at the 19th Conference of Caribbean Studies Association, Mexico, May 1994. 19 p.

     Music/ Popular music/ Dance hall music/ Reggae music/ Image of women/ Lyrics/ Sexuality

22   _____. "Something Ancestral Recaptured: Spirit Possession as Trope in Selected Feminist Fictions of the African Diaspora." In *Motherlands, Black Women's Writing from Africa, the Caribbean and South Asia,* edited by Susheila Nasta, p. 64–87. New Brunswick: Rutgers University Press, 1992.
     Spirit possession/ Erna Brodber/ Sylvia Wynter/ Una Marson/ Myalism/ Authors (UWIM)

23   _____. "Words Unbroken by the Beat: the Performance Poetry of Jean Binta Breeze and Mikey Smith." *Wasafiri.* No. 11 (1990): 7–13.
     Dub poetry/ Jean Breeze/ Poets (UWIM)

24   _____. "Writing Oral History, Sistren Theatre Collective's *Lionheart Gal.*" *Kunapipi.* Vol. 11, no. 1 (1989): 49–57.
     Sistren Theatre Collective/ Oral history/ *Lionheart Gal*/ Life stories (UWIM)

25   Craig, Dawnette R. "Woman as Mother in Selected Works of West Indian Drama." Master's thesis, University of the West Indies, 1986. 55 leaves.
     Study of Derek Walcott's *Ti-Jean and His Brothers*; Errol John's *Moon on a Rainbow Shawl*; Eric Roach's *Belle Fanto;* and Trevor Rhone's *Old Story Time* and *Two Can Play.*
     Mother in literature/ *Old Story Time*/ *Two Can Play* (UWIM)

26 Dance, Daryl Cumber. "Go Eena Kumbla: a Comparison of Erna Brodber's *Jane and Louisa Will Soon Come Home* and Toni Cade Bambara's *The Salt Eaters*." In *Caribbean Women Writers: Essays from the First International Conference,* edited by Selwyn R. Cudjoe, p. 169–84. Wellesley, Mass.: Calaloux Publications, 1990.
Erna Brodber/ *Jane and Louisa/* Authors (UWIM)

27 Dawes, Kwame (Neville). "Violence and the Position of Race, Class, Religion and Gender in Jamaican Fiction and Drama." PhD thesis, University of New Brunswick, 1992. 661 p.
Violence/ Race/ Religion/ Women in literature (UWIM)

28 Fido, Elaine Savory. "Finding a Way to Tell It: Methodology and Commitment in Theatre about Women in Barbados and Jamaica." In *Out of the Kumbla: Caribbean Women and Literature,* edited by Carol Boyce Davies and Elaine Savory Fido, p. 331–43. New Jersey: Africa World Press, 1990.
Theatre (UWIM)

29 Ford-Smith, Honor. "The Case of Iris Armstrong: a Forum for Women in Sugar." *Third World Popular Theatre Newsletter* (Caribbean edition). Issue no. 3 (1983): 22–25.
Sistren Theatre Collective/ Psychodrama (UWIM)

30 _____. "Ring-ding in a Tight Corner: a Case Study of Funding and Organizational Democracy in Sistren, 1977–1988." Toronto: ICAE, 1989. 107 p.
Examines factors that limit the impact of women's organizations in Jamaica. Focuses on Sistren Theatre Collective giving an account of its history in the context of political and cultural boundaries, its sources of funding and difficulties in maintaining financial leverage. Looks at structural problems and concludes with recommendations for future development.
Sistren Theatre Collective/ Women's organizations/ Financial aid/ Funding agencies (UWIM)

31 _____. "Sistren." *Fuse: the Cultural News Magazine.* (1981): 246–51.
Sistren Theatre Collective/ Theatre (UWIM)

32 _____. "Sistren at Work." *Carib.* No. 4 (1986): 55–74.
Briefly describes how Sistren uses drama through its workshop programme to solve women's problems. An excerpt from

"Domestick" and a " Tribute to Gloria Who Overcame Death" are included.
Sistren Theatre Collective/ Theatre/ Psychodrama (UWIM)

33 _____. "Sistren: Exploring Women's Problems Through Drama." *Jamaica Journal.* Vol. 19, no. 1 (1986): 2–12.
Sistren Theatre Collective/ Theatre/ Psychodrama (UWIM)

34 _____. "Sistren: Jamaican Women's Theatre." In *Cultures in Contention,* edited by Douglas Kahn and Dion Neumeier, p. 85–91. Seattle: Real Comet Press, 1985.
Sistren Theatre Collective/ Theatre (STC)

35 _____. "Sistren Women's Theatre: a Model for Consciousness-raising." In *Journey in the Shaping: Report of the First Symposium of Women in Caribbean Culture, July 24, 1981*, edited by Margaret Hope, p. 52–59. Barbados: Wand, 1981.
Sistren Theatre Collective/ Theatre/ Consciousness-raising (UWIM)

36 _____. "Sistren Women's Theatre: Organizing and Conscientization." In *Women of the Caribbean,* edited by Pat Ellis, p. 122–28. Kingston: Kingston Publishers, 1986.
Sistren Theatre Collective/ Theatre/ Consciousness-raising (UWIM)

37 Francis-Hinds, Suzanne. "Edna Manley." *Arts Jamaica.* Vol. 1, no. 2 (1982): 2–4.
Edna Manley/ Biographical data/ Artists/ Sculptors (UWIM)

38 Fraser, Lorna A. "Literature, Self and Society: the Ontological Dilemma in *Wuthering Heights, Tender is the Night* and *Myal.*" Master's thesis, University of the West Indies, 1992. 90 leaves.
Self-concept in literature/ Erna Brodber/ *Myal*/ Emily Brontë/ F. Scott Fitzgerald/ Sense of being/ Authors (UWIM)

39 French, Joan. "Organizing Women Through Drama in Rural Jamaica." *Ideas in Action.* No. 163 (1985): 3–7.
Rural women/ Sistren Theatre Collective/ Consciousness-raising/ Theatre (UWIM)

40 Gonzalez, Anson. "A New Important Voice in Caribbean Poetry: Olive Senior's *Talking of Trees.*" *The New Voices.* Vol 14, no. 28 (1986): 31–34.
Olive Senior/ Poets/ Authors (UWIM)

41 Griffin, Gabriele. "Writing the Body: Reading Joan Riley, Grace Nichols and Ntozake Shange." In *Black Women's Writing*, edited by Gina Wisker, p. 55–77. New York: St Martin's Press, 1992.
Joan Riley/ *Unbelonging*/ Authors (UWIM)

42 Hamilton, Marlene. "Attitudes of Jamaican Adolescents to Popular Dance Hall Music." Paper presented at the 14th Conference of the Caribbean Studies Association, Barbados, May 23–26, 1989. 18 p.
Adolescents/ Dance hall music/ Music/ Image of women/ Attitudes (UWIM)

43 Hewitt, Mary Jane C. "A Comparative Study of the Careers of Zora Neale Hurston and Louise Bennett as Cultural Conservators." PhD thesis, University of the West Indies, 1989. 691 leaves.
Included in this study are a chronology of Louise Bennett, a listing of Little Theatre pantomimes in which she played a role, titles of songs and music written by her for pantomimes, a list of published, unpublished works and performances, as well as critical studies of Louise Bennett's works.
Louise Bennett/ Folklore/ Theatre/ Radio programmes/ Dialect poetry/ Pantomimes/ Cultural heritage (UWIM)

44 Hope, Margaret. *Journey in the Shaping: Report of the First Symposium on Women in Caribbean Culture, July 24, 1981.* Barbados: WAND, 1981. 59 p.
Culture/ Image of women/ Performers/ Performing arts/ Sistren Theatre Collective/ Artists (UWIM)

45 Insanally, Annette. "Eroticism: the Consciousness of Self as Seen in R. Ferre's *Fabulas de la Garza Desangrada* and Lorna Goodison's *Tamarind Season*." *Caribbean Literature in Comparison*: Papers presented at 8th Conference on Spanish Caribbean Literature, 9–11 April, 1985, edited by Joe Pereira, p.73–82. Kingston: University of the West Indies, Institute of Caribbean Studies, 1990.
Sexuality/ Eroticism/ Lorna Goodison/ Poets/ *Tamarind Season*/ Self-concept in literature (UWIM)

46 Johnson, Joyce. "Autobiography, History and the Novel: Erna Brodber's *Jane and Louisa Will Soon Come Home*." *Journal of West Indian Literature*. Vol. 3, no. 1 (1989): 47–59.
Erna Brodber/ *Jane and Louisa*/ Autobiography/ History/ Social development/ Authors (UWIM)

47 _____. "Finding a Literary Medium: Jean D'Costa's Novels for Children." *Wasafari*. No. 5 (1986): 12–15.
Jean D'Costa/ Children's literature/ Authors (UWIM)

48 _____. "*Myal*: Text and Context." *Journal of West Indian Literature*. Vol. 5, nos. 1–2 (1992): 48–64.
Erna Brodber/ *Myal*/ Authors (UWIM)

49 Jones, Jennifer. "Seminar Paper on the Situation of Female Participation in Cultural Development in Jamaica, Obstacles to their Full Participation and Recommendations to Further their Future Participation," Paper ... for the International Seminar on Measures to Encourage the Participation of Women in Cultural Development, held in Oslo, Norway, March 30–April 2, 1987, organized by the Norwegian National Commission for UNESCO, in cooperation with UNESCO. 17 leaves.
Cultural development/ Women's role (STC)

50 Liddell, Janice Lee. "The Narrow Enclosure of Motherdom/Martyrdom: a Study of Gatha Randall Barton in Sylvia Wynter's *The Hills of Hebron*." In *Out of the Kumbla: Caribbean Women and Literature*, edited by Carole Boyce Davies and Elaine Savory Fido, p. 321–30. New Jersey: Africa World Press, 1990.
Sylvia Wynter/ Mother in literature/ Authors/ *Hills of Hebron* (UWIM)

51 Lovindeer, Lloyd. "Women in Dancehall: a Response." *Jamaica Journal*. Vol. 23, no. 1 (1990): 51–52.
Music/ Dance hall music/ Popular culture/ Sexuality/ Image of women/ Lyrics/ Popular music (UWIM)

52 McCaffrey, Kathleen M. *Images of Women in the Literature of Selected Developing Countries: Ghana, Senegal, Haiti, Jamaica*. Washington, D.C.: US AID, Office of Women in Development, 1978. 229 p.
Image of women/ Culture/ Perception/ Women in literature (UWIM)

53 McIntosh, Sandy. "From the Street to the Boards." *Unicef News*. Issue 104/1980/2: 18–19.
Sistren Theatre Collective/ Theatre (UWIM)

54 Mordecai, Pamela. "Into the Beautiful Garden: Some Comments on Erna Brodber's *Jane and Louisa Will Soon Come Home.*" *Caribbean Quarterly.* Vol 29, no. 2 (1983): 44–53.
Erna Brodber/ *Jane and Louisa*/ Authors (UWIM)

55 _____. "Wooing with Words: Some Comments on the Poetry of Lorna Goodison." *Jamaica Journal.* Vol. 45 (1981): 44–56.
Lorna Goodison/ Poets (UWIM)

56 Morris, Ann R., and Margaret Dunn. "The Bloodstream of Our Inheritance: Female Identity and the Caribbean Mothers' land." In *Motherlands, Black Women's Writing from Africa, the Caribbean and South Asia,* edited by Susheila Nasta, p. 219–37. New Brunswick: Rutgers University Press, 1992.
Mother in literature/ Motherland/ Michelle Cliff/ *No Telephone to Heaven*/ Authors/ Identity (UWIM)

57 Morris, Mervyn. "Gender in *Summer Lightning* and *Talking of Trees.*" Paper presented at First Disciplinary Seminar, Gender Issues in the Humanities, held by Women and Development Studies/ Faculty of Arts and General Studies, UWI, St. Augustine, Trinidad, 4–9 September, 1988. 11 p.
Olive Senior/ *Summer Lightning*/ *Talking of Trees*/ Authors (UWIM)

58 _____. "Louise Bennett in Print." *Caribbean Quarterly.* Vol. 28, nos. 1 & 2 (1982): 44–56.
Louise Bennett/ Poets/ Dialect poetry (UWIM)

59 _____. "On Reading Louise Bennett Seriously." *Jamaica Journal.* Vol. 1, no. 1 (1967): 69–74.
Louise Bennett/ Poets/ Dialect poetry (UWIM)

60 Nicholson, Hilary. "Sharing Experiences: the Sistren Theatre Collective." *Womenshare Funding Newsnote.* Issue 1 (1988): 3–6.
Sistren Theatre Collective/ Theatre (UWIM)

61 Noel, Keith. "Art as Protest: the Work of Sistren Theatre Collective in Jamaica." Master's thesis, University of the West Indies, 1988. 91 leaves.
Sistren Theatre Collective/ Conscioiusness-raising/ Theatre (UWIM)

62 O'Callaghan, Evelyn. "Engineering the Female Subject: Erna Brodber's *Myal*." *Kunapipi*. Vol. 12, no. 3 (1990): 93–103.
Erna Brodber/ *Myal/* Authors (UWIM)

63 _____. "Feminist Consciousness: European/American Theory, Jamaican Stories." *Sargasso*. Special issue (1988): 27–51.
Authors/ Olive Senior/ Hazel Campbell/ Sistren Theatre Collective/ Opal Adisa Palmer/ Feminist theory/ Feminist literary criticism (UWIM)

64 _____. "Rediscovering the Natives of My Person, Review Article on Erna Brodber's *Jane and Louisa Will Soon Come Home*." *Jamaica Journal*. Vol.16, no. 3 (1983): 61–64.
Erna Brodber/ *Jane and Louisa/* Authors (UWIM)

65 Paravisini-Gebert, Lizabeth. "*The White Witch of Rosehall* and the Legitimacy of Female Power in the Caribbean Plantation." *Journal of West Indian Literature*. Vol. 4, no. 2 (1990): 25–45.
Annie Palmer/ Woman power in literature/ Legends (UWIM)

66 Pollard, Velma. "An Introduction to the Poetry of Olive Senior." *Callaloo*. Vol. 11, no. 3 (1988): 540–46.
Authors/ Olive Senior/ Poets/ Style (UWIM)

67 _____. "Mothertongue Voices in the Writing of Olive Senior and Lorna Goodison." In *Motherlands: Black Women's Writing from Africa, the Caribbean and South Asia,* edited by Susheila Nasta, p. 238–53. New Brunswick: Rutgers University Press, 1992.
Language/ Lorna Goodison/ Olive Senior/ Mother tongue/ Code switching/ Poets/ Authors (UWIM)

68 _____. "Olive Senior: Journalist, Researcher, Poet, Fiction Writer." *Callaloo*. Vol. 11, no. 3 (1988): 479.
Olive Senior/ Journalists/ Poets/ Authors (UWIM)

69 Poupeye-Rammelaere, Veerle. "The Role of Women in the Development of Jamaican Art." Kingston: Frame Centre Gallery, 1994. 8 p.
Art history/ Women in art development/ Artists (UWIM)

70 Rugg, Akua. "Sistren is Something Else." *Race Today Review*. (1984): 30–31, 32.
Sistren Theatre Collective/ Theatre (UWIM)

71   Sandmann, M. "Dorothy Payne: a Newcomer to Sculpture." *Caribbean Quarterly.* Vol. 5, no. 4 (1959): 229–30.
        Dorothy Payne/ Sculptors (UWIM)

72   Shields, Kathryn. "Gender Discourse and the Language of Control." Paper presented at the First Disciplinary Seminar, Gender Issues in the Humanities, held by Women and Development Studies/ Faculty of Arts and General Studies, UWI, St Augustine, September 4–9, 1988. 12 p.
        Language/ Speech patterns/ Discourse strategy/ Radio talk shows (UWIM)

73   Sistren Theatre Collective. "Women's Theatre in Jamaica." *Grassroots Development.* Vol. 7, no. 3 (1983): 44–52.
        Theatre/ Sistren Theatre Collective (UWIM)

74   Smilowitz, Erika. "Weary of Life and All My Heart's Dull Pain: the Poetry of Una Marson." In *Critical Issues in West Indian Literature: Selected Papers from West Indian Literature Conferences, 1981–1983,* edited by Erika Smilowitz and Roberta Knowles, p. 19–32. Parkesburg, Iowa: Caribbean Books, 1983.
        Una Marson/ Poets (UWIM)

75   Smith, Jean. "The Woman as Artist: a Historical Perspective." *Arts Jamaica: A Quarterly of the Visual Arts.* Vol. 1, no. 2 (1982): 5–9.
        Artists/ Women in art development/ Art history (UWIM)

76   "Theatre of the People: Reaching the Masses with Drama: Sistren and Pat Cumper." In *Theatre,* edited by Judy S. Stone, p. 59–79. Basingstoke: Macmillan, 1994.
        Pat Cumper/ Sistren Theatre Collective/ Conscioiusness-raising/ Theatre (UWIM)

77   Wint-Bauer, Valrie. "Dub Poet Rooted in Reality." *Race Today.* Vol. 16, no. 2 (1984): 25.
        Dub poetry/ Jean Breeze/ Poets (UWIM)

78   Woodcock, Bruce. "Long Memoried Women: Caribbean Women Poets." In *Black Women's Writing,* edited by Gina Wisker, p. 55–77. New York: St Martin's Press, 1992.
        Louise Bennett/ Elean Thomas/ Jean Breeze/ Lorna Goodison/ Christine Craig/ Poets (UWIM)

Biography, Interviews, and Personal Narratives 79-125

Biographies, autobiographies, oral histories, diaries form an important genre for research in women's studies. These are listed here, jointly with a number of interviews which provide insights into the character and society of the time from the point of view of little known as well as well-known Jamaican women.

79 Alexander, Ziggi and Audrey Dewjee. *Mary Seacole: Jamaican National Heroine and "Doctress" in the Crimean War.* London: Brent Library Series, 1982. 12 p.
    Mary Seacole/ Nursing/ Philanthropy/ Travel/ Freed women (UWIM)

80 Ballysingh, Harold R. *Quaker Lady in Jamaica: a Memoir of My Wife.* Kingston: The Author, 1983. 104 p.
    Marion Ballysingh/ Social workers/ Quakers/ Council for Voluntary Social Service/ Social services (NLJ)

81 Bennett, Louise. "Bennett on Bennett." Interview by Dennis Scott. *Caribbean Quarterly.* Vol. 29, no. 2 (1968): 22–29.
    Louise Bennett/ Poets/ Dialect poetry (UWIM)

82 Breeze, Jean. "An Interview with Jean Breeze." *Commonwealth: Essays and Studies.* Vol. 8, no. 2 (1986): 51–58.
    Jean Breeze/ Dub poetry/ Poets (UWIM)

83 Brodber, Erna. "Fiction in the Scientific Procedure." In *Caribbean Women Writers: Essays from the First International Conference,*

edited by Selwyn R. Cudjoe, p. 51–60. Wellesley, Mass.: Calaloux Publications, 1990.
Self-assessment/ Erna Brodber (UWIM)

84 _____. "The Pioneering of Miss Bailey." *Jamaica Journal.* Vol. 19, no. 2 (1986): 9–14.
Amy Bailey/ Social workers/ Teachers (UWIM)

85 Brown, Rosemary. *Being Brown: a Very Public Life.* Toronto: Random House, 1989. 248 p.
Rosemary Brown/ Political participation/ Social action/ Canada/ Legislators/ Migration/ Autobiography/ Leadership (UWIM)

86 Brown, Wayne. *Edna Manley: the Private Years, 1900–1938.* London: Deutsch, 1972. 264 p.
Edna Manley/ Artists/ Sculptors (UWIM)

87 Chang, Victor. "Sylvia Wynter (1928–)." In *Fifty Caribbean Writers: a Bio-bibliographical Critical Sourcebook,* edited by Daryl Cumber Dance, p. 35–45. New York: Greenwood Press, 1986.
Sylvia Wynter/ Authors (UWIM)

88 "Charles Lionel James Interview with Amy Jacques Garvey." In *Footsoldiers of the Universal Negro Improvement Association (their own words),* by Jeanette Smith-Irwin, p. 84–91. Trenton, NJ: Africa World Press, 1989.
Amy Jacques Garvey/ UNIA/ Garvey Movement/ Black nationalism (UWIM)

89 Cooper, Afua. "Finding My Voice." In *Caribbean Women Writers: Essays from the First International Conference,* edited by Selwyn R. Cudjoe, p. 301–305. Wellesley, Mass.: Calaloux Publications, 1990.
Self-assessment/ Afua Cooper (UWIM)

90 Craddock, Sally. *Retired Except on Demand: the Life of Dr Cicely Williams.* Oxford: Green College, 1983. 198 p.
Women in medicine/ Cicely Williams (UWIM)

91 Crosdale, Al. "The Superlative Ms. Lou." *West Indian Digest.* No. 101 (1983): 42–46.
Louise Bennett/ Poets (UWIM)

92 Craig, Christine. *"Wonderful Adventures of Mrs Seacole in Many Lands*: Autobiography as Literary Genre and a Window to Character." *Caribbean Quarterly.* Vol. 30, no. 2 (1984): 33–47.
Mary Seacole/ Autobiography/ History/ Freed women/ Travel (UWIM)

93 "Debbie Pinks: President of Women Inc." *Money Index.* No. 341 (1992): 42–43.
Debbie Pinks/ Women Inc./ Women's Trade Fair (UWIM)

94 Ebanks, Roderick. "Ma Lou and the Afro-Jamaican Pottery Tradition." *Jamaica Journal.* Vol. 17, no. 3 (1984): 31–37.
Potters/ African influences/ Pottery techniques/ Louisa Jones

95 Ford-Smith, Honor. *Una Marson: Black Nationalist and Feminist Writer.* Kingston: Sistren, 1986. 27 p.
Una Marson/ Poets/ Black nationalism/ Feminism/ "Pocomania" (UWIM)

96 Garvey, Amy Jacques. *Why Mrs Garvey Refused the $6,800 Pension.* Kingston: Abeng, 1973. 9 p.
Amy Jacques Garvey/ Pensions/ (UWIM)

97 Gloudon, Barbara. "Hon. Lady Bustamante, O. J. Interviewed." *Jamaica Journal.* Vol. 17, no. 4 (1984–1985): 24–31.
Gladys Bustamante/ Political participation/ (UWIM)

98 _____. "Hon. Louise Bennett, O. J.: Fifty Years of Laughter." *Jamaica Journal.* Vol. 19, no. 3 (1986): 2–10.
Louise Bennett/ Poets/ Dialect poetry (UWIM)

99 "Gloria Escoffery Talks with Alex Gradusov." *Jamaica Journal.* Vol. 5, no. 1 (1971): 34–40.
Gloria Escoffery/ Artists (UWIM)

100 "Gloria Knight: Mutual Life's Bright No-nonsense President Still Has Worlds to Conquer." *Money Index.* No. 270 (1991): 14–15, 19–20, 26.
Gloria Knight/ Mutual Life Insurance Company/ Executives/ Women in business/ Leadership (UWIM)

101 Goodison, Lorna. " How I Became a Writer." In *Caribbean Women Writers: Essays from the First International Conference,* edited by

Selwyn R. Cudjoe, p. 290–93. Wellesley, Mass.: Calaloux Publications, 1990.

Lorna Goodison/ Self-assessment/ Poets (UWIM)

102 Guy, Henry A. and Lavern Bailey, eds. *Women of Distinction in Jamaica: a Record of Career Women in Jamaica, their Background, Service and Achievements.* Kingston: Caribbean Herald Associates, 1977. 164 p.

Collective biography/ Professionals (UWIM)

103 Haniff, Nesha. *Blaze of Fire: Significant Contributions of Caribbean Women.* Toronto, Ontario: Sister Vision, 1988. 220 p.

Among the women described are three Jamaicans: Louise Bennett, poet, Mabel Tenn, businesswoman, and Esmine Antoine, higgler.

Collective biography/ Louise Bennett/ Mabel Tenn/ Esmine Antoine/ Development/ Poets/ Women in business/ Higglering/ Leadership (UWIM)

104 Johnson, Joyce. "Jean D'Costa (1937–)." In *Fifty Caribbean Writers: a Bio-bibliographical Critical Sourcebook,* edited by Daryl Cumber Dance, p 160–65. New York: Greenwood Press, 1986.

Jean D'Costa/ Children's literature/ Authors (UWIM)

105 Josephs, Aleric. "Mary Seacole: Her Life and Times." Master's thesis, University of the West Indies, 1985. 111 leaves.

Mary Seacole/ History/ Nursing/ Travel/ Freed women (UWIM)

106 "Interview with the Hon. Portia Simpson." *Money Index.* No. 312 (1992): 7–8.

Portia Simpson/ Political participation/ Leadership (UWIM)

107 Lewis, Rupert, and Maureen Warner Lewis. "Amy Jacques Garvey." *Jamaica Journal.* Vol. 20, no. 3 (1987): 39–43.

Amy Jacques Garvey/ Black nationalism/ Garvey Movement (UWIM)

108 MacLeavy, Jennifer Brown. "Amy Beckford Bailey: a Biography." *Jamaican Historical Review.* Vol. 18 (1993): 31–39.

Also presented as a postgraduate seminar paper to the Department of History, University of the West Indies (Mona, Jamaica).

Amy Bailey/ Social workers/ Teachers/ Women's Liberal Club/ Housecraft Training Centre/ Social action (UWIM)

109 Manley, Edna. *Edna Manley: the Diaries,* edited by Rachel Manley, Kingston: Heinemann Publishers, 1989. 308 p.
Edna Manley/ Sculptors/ Diaries/ Artists (UWIM)

110 Martin, Tony. "Amy Ashwood Garvey: Wife no. 1." *Jamaica Journal.* Vol. 20, no. 3 (1987): 32–36.
Amy Ashwood Garvey/ Black nationalism/ Garvey Movement (UWIM)

111 McDonnough, Maxine. "Sister Samad: Living the Garvey Life." *Jamaica Journal.* Vol. 20, no. 3 (1987): 77–84.
Sister Mariamme Samad/ Garvey Movement/ Black nationalism (UWIM)

112 McFarlane, B. "Edna Manley Interview." *Jamaica Journal.* Vol. 4, no. 1 (1970): 33–37.
Edna Manley/ Sculptors/ Artists (UWIM)

113 Morris, Mervyn. "Louise Bennett (1919–)." In *Fifty Caribbean Writers: a Bio-bibliographical Critical Sourcebook,* edited by Daryl Cumber Dance, p. 35–45. New York: Greenwood Press, 1986.
Louise Bennett/ Poets (UWIM)

114 Nugent, Maria. *Lady Nugent's Journal of Her Residence in Jamaica from 1801–1805.* Revised by Philip Wright. Kingston: Institute of Jamaica, 1966. 331 p.
Diaries/ Colonial society/ Social conditions/ Plantation society/ Maria Nugent (UWIM)

115 O'Callaghan, Evelyn. "Erna Brodber (1940–)." In *Fifty Caribbean Writers: a Bio-bibliographical Critical Sourcebook,* edited by Daryl Cumber Dance, p. 71–82. New York: Greenwood Press, 1986.
Erna Brodber/ Authors (UWIM)

116 O'Gorman, Pamela. "Marjorie Whylie's Contribution to the Development of Drumming in Jamaica." *Jamaica Journal.* Vol. 24, no. 1 (1991): 33–37.
Marjorie Whylie/ Drumming/ Music/ African influences/ Musicians (UWIM)

117 Prince, Nancy. *A Black Woman's Odyssey Through Russia and Jamaica: the Narrative of Nancy Prince.* Introduction by Ronald G.Walters. New York: Markus Wiener, 1990. 93 p.

Nancy Prince a free black woman born in 1799 writes about her childhood in Massachusetts, her nine and one half years in Russia and her missionary work in Jamaica from 1840–1843.

Nancy Prince/ Freed women/ History/ Missionary work/ Travel/ Autobiography (UWIM)

118 Robinson, Amy. "Authority and Public Display of Identity: Wonderful Adventures of Mrs Seacole in Many Lands." *Feminist Studies.* Vol. 20, no. 3 (1994): 537–57.

Mary Seacole/ Identity/ Freed women/ Autobiography (UWIM)

119 Rowell, Charles H. "An Interview with Olive Senior." *Callaloo.* Vol. 11, no. 3 (1988): 480–90.

Olive Senior/ Authors/ Poets (UWIM)

120 Rutherford, Anna. "Interview with Olive Senior." *Kunapipi.* Vol 8, no. 2 (1986): 11–20.

Olive Senior/ Poets/ Authors (UWIM)

121 Seacole, Mary. *Wonderful Adventures of Mrs Seacole in Many Lands,* edited by Ziggi Alexander and Audrey Dewjee. Bristol: Falling Wall Press, 1984. 274, [16] p.

Mary Seacole/ Freed women/ Autobiography/ Travel/ Nursing

122 Silvera, Makeda. *Silenced: Talks with Working Class Caribbean Women about their Lives as Domestic Workers in Canada.* Toronto: Sister Vision, 1989. 114 p.

Personal testimony of women domestic workers from the West Indies. Four of the ten women are Jamaicans. Gives an account of how women perceive the work they do and their interactions with their employers and the state.

Domestic workers/ Oral history/ Canada/ Socioeconomic status/ Life stories/ Working class women/ Migration/ Sexual harassment (UWIM)

123 Sistren Theatre Collective with Honor Ford-Smith. *Lionheart Gal: Life Studies of Jamaican Women.* London: The Women's Press, 1986. 298 p.

Life stories/ Motherhood/ Sexuality/ Migration/ Domestic violence/ Sistren Theatre Collective/ Working class women/ Oral history/ Nanny (UWIM)

124 Smilowitz, Erika. "Una Marson: Woman Before Her Time." *Jamaica Journal.* Vol. 16, no. 2 (1983): 62–68.

Una Marson/ Poets/ Social workers/ Black nationalism (UWIM)

125 Vassell, Linnette. *Voices of Women in Jamaica, 1898–1938.* Kingston: University of the West Indies, Department of History, 1993. 45 p.

Gives brief biographical data on women involved in political and social activism. Includes views of these women expressed in newspapers such as the *Jamaica Advocate, Public Opinion* and the *Daily Gleaner* and in magazines of the period.

Collective biography/ Political views/ Social views/ Public opinion (UWIM)

Economic Conditions and Employment   126-233

This has proven, by the quantity of material located, to be the area of greatest research emphasis on women in Jamaica. Works here document women's involvement in agriculture and the labour market, and discuss the debt crisis and the effect of structural adjustment on women. Women as heads of households, household income and women in the informal sector are also highlighted.

126 Aitken-Soux, Percy. *Rural Women Survey: Survey of Women and Small Farms 0–5 Acres of "Philogrip" Project Southern Trelawny, Jamaica.* Kingston: IICA/Jamaica, 1980. 3 v.
      Rural women/ Small farms/ Agriculture/ Trelawny/ Philogrip Project (UWIM)

127 Alleyne, Sylvan, Scarlette Gillings, and Lebert Lawrence. "Profile of the Impact Worker in Kingston, Jamaica." In *Contemporary Caribbean: a Sociological Reader*, edited by Susan Craig, p. 111–25. Port of Spain: The Author, 1982. Vol. 2.
      Describes the special works programme introduced by the People's National Party government in 1974 to cope with some of the unemployment problems. Looks at the programme in the Kingston and St Andrew area where the majority of the workers were women.
      Impact Programme/ Special Employment Programme/ Employment opportunities/ Government programmes (UWIM)

128 Anderson, Patricia. "Protection and Oppression: a Case Study of Domestic Service in Jamaica." Paper presented at the Second Disciplinary Seminar, Women and Development Studies: Social Sciences: Barbados, 3–7 April, 1989. 31 p.

Also published in *Labour, Capital and Society*. Vol. 20, no. 1 (1991): 10–39.

Informal sector/ Domestic workers/ Labour relations/ Working conditions/ Kingston/ Worker employer relationship/ Sexual harassment (UWIM)

129 Anderson-Manley, Beverly. "Gender Considerations in Policy Design." *Money Index*. No. 341 (1992): 19–21.

Summary of a paper presented at the UNDP/PIOJ Seminar, Preparing for the 21st Century, 6–7 October, 1992. 16 leaves.

Paper includes: "Gender Monitoring Checklist" by Bureau of Women's Affairs. Also published in *Jamaica: Preparing for the 21st Century*, edited by Patsy Lewis, p. 171–80. Kingston: Ian Randle Publishers, 1994.

Status/ Government policy/ Bureau of Women's Affairs/ Development planning (UWIM)

130 Antrobus, Peggy, and Barbara Rogers. "Hanover Street: Jamaican Women in Welding and Woodworking." *Women's Studies International: A Supplement to Women's Studies Quarterly*. No. 1 (1982): 10–14.

Development projects/ Bureau of Women's Affairs/ Training programmes/ Skills training/ Welding/ Woodworking/ Non-traditional occupations (UWIM)

131 Blackwood, Florette. "Performance of Men and Women in the Repayment of Mortgage Loans in Jamaica." In *Learning about Women and Urban Services in Latin America and the Caribbean: a Report on the Women Low-income Households and Urban Services Project of the Population Council*, edited by Marianne Schmink, Judith Bruce and Marilyn Kohn, p. 101–15. Washington, D.C.: Population Council, 1986.

The original 84-page study conducted in 1983 and sponsored by the Urban Development Corporation is in the collection of the ISER Documentation Centre.

Housing/ Mortgages/ Loan repayment/ Home ownership (UDC and ISER)

132 Blake-Nelson, Hazel. "Action Taken by the Jamaica Women's Bureau to Create Employment Opportunities for Women". Paper presented at the ILO Symposium in Brussels, November, 1977. 23 p.

Bureau of Women's Affairs/ Employment opportunities/ Development planning. (WB)

133 Bolles, Augusta Lynn. "Economic Crisis and Female-headed Households in Urban Jamaica." In *Women and Change in Latin America*, edited by June Nash and Helen I. Safa, p. 65–83. South Hadley, MA.: Bergen and Garvey, 1986.

Household income/ Female headed households/ Working class women/ Survival strategies/ Urban women (UWIM)

134 _____. "Household Economic Strategies in Kingston, Jamaica." In *Women and World Change: Equity Issues in Development*, edited by Naomi Black and Ann Baker Cottrell, p. 83–96. California: Sage, 1981.

Informal sector/ Urban women/ Working class women/ Female headed households/ Household income/ Poor/ Survival strategies (UWIM)

135 _____. "IMF Destabilization, the Impact on Jamaican Working Class Women." *TransAfrica Forum*. Vol. 2, no. 1 (1983): 63–75.

International Monetary Fund/ Working class women/ Debt crisis/ Female headed households/ Survival strategies/ Household income (UWIM)

136 _____. "The Impact of Working Class Women's Employment on Household Organization in Kingston, Jamaica." PhD thesis, Rutgers University, 1981. 265 p.

Working class women/ Female headed households/ Urban women (UWIM)

137 _____. "Kitchens Hit by Priorities: Employed Jamaican Working Class Women Confront the IMF." In *Women, Men and the International Division of Labour*, edited by June Nash and Patricia M. Fernandez, p. 138–60. New York: SUNY, 1983.

International Monetary Fund/ Working class women/ Urban women/ Manufacturing sector/ Household income/ Debt crisis/ Survival strategies/ Female headed households (UWIM)

138 Brown, Janet, and Melrose Rattray. "Women in Jamaican Development: an Overview Report Towards Development Strategies." Prepared for CIDA, Canadian High Commission, Kingston, Jamaica. 1987. 107, 10 p.
Development planning/ Socioeconomic status/ Women's role (UWIM)

139 Burgess, Judith A. "Women's Migration and Work: the Integration of Caribbean Women into the New York City Nurse Workforce." PhD thesis, Columbia University, 1989. 474 p.
Thesis focuses on nurses from Jamaica, Barbados, Trinidad and Tobago and Guyana.
Migration/ Nurses/ New York City/ Status/ Labour supply/ Socioeconomic status/ Educational attainment (UWIM)

140 *Caribbean Resource Book Focussing on Women in Development.* Collaborative Effort on the Part of the Women's Bureau of Jamaica, Extra-Mural Department, UWI, and the International Women's Tribune Centre. New York: International Women's Tribune Centre, [1977]. 213 p.
Provides information on projects, organizations, publications, funding sources and possibilities for action involving women. Jamaican organizations are listed on p. 46–72.
Women's organizations/ Development projects/ Funding agencies (UWIM)

141 Celestine, Sharon, and A. Blackwood-Harriott. "Women in Professional Services: a Gender Perspective of Female Entrepreneurs in the Service Sector for Small and Micro Enterprises in Jamaica." 1993. [112] p.
Prepared for the Government of Jamaica/Government of the Netherlands Microenterprise Project.
Small business/ Professionals/ Entrepreneurs/ Women in business/ Data processing industry (ISER)

142 Chaney, Elsa M. "Scenarios of Hunger in the Caribbean: Migration Decline of Small-holders Agriculture and the Feminization of Farming." Michigan: Michigan State University, 1983. Working paper no. 18. 30 p.
Small farms/ Agriculture/ Rural women/ Nutrition/ Food supply (ISER)

143 _____, and Martha W. Lewis. *Creating a Women's Component: a Case Study in Rural Jamaica*. Washington, D.C.: USAID, Office of Women in Development, 1981. 35 p.

Development projects/ Agriculture/ Small farms/ Food production/ Nutrition/ Rural development/ Integrated Rural Development Project/ Rural women (PIOJ)

144 Cuthbert, Marlene. "Survey of Women Professionals in the Electronic Media." In *Women and Media Decision-making in the Caribbean*, edited by Marlene Cuthbert, p. 204–14. Kingston: CARIMAC, University of the West Indies, 1982.

Broadcasting industry/ Professionals/ Women in the media/ Radio programmes/ Television programmes (UWIM)

145 D'Amico-Samuels, Deborah. "You Can't Get Me Out of the Race: Women and Economic Development in Negril, Jamaica, West Indies". PhD thesis, City University of New York. 1986. 371 p.

Tourist industry/ Negril/ Development/ Entrepreneurs/ Colour/ Class/ Rural women (ISER)

146 Davies, Omar, and Patricia Anderson. "The Impact of the Recession and Adjustment Policies on Poor Urban Women in Jamaica." Prepared for the United Nations Children's Fund. 1987. 61 leaves.

Also presented as a paper at the 14th Conference of the Caribbean Studies Association, Barbados, May 23–27, 1989. Paper entitled "The Impact of Recession and Structural Adjustment Policies on Poor Urban Women in Jamaica." 43 p.

Urban women/ Poor/ Household income/ Living conditions/ Structural adjustment (ISER)

147 Davies, Rose. *Women as the Recipients of Services from Resources Allocation in the National Budget of Jamaica*. Port of Spain: UNECLAC, 1986. 91 p.

Status/ Participation/ Social services/ Health care services/ Educational opportunities/ Employment opportunities/ National budget/ Sex role stereotyping/ Development planning (ISER)

148 "The Debt Crisis and Women in Jamaica." In *Women and World Economic Crisis*, edited by Jeanne Vickers, p. 99–103. London: Zed Books, 1991.

Debt crisis/ Structural adjustment/ Household income (UWIM)

149 Dunn, Leith. *Women Organizing for Change in the Caribbean Free Zone: Strategies and Methods*. The Hague: Institute of Social Studies, 1991. 31 p.

Paper focuses on free zone workers in Jamaica and the Dominican Republic.

Free zone workers/ Working conditions/ Worker employee relationship/ Dominican Republic (UWIM)

150 Durant-Gonzalez, Victoria. "The Occupation of Higglering." *Jamaica Journal*. Vol. 16, no. 3 (1983): 2–12.

Informal sector/ Higglering/ Market vendors/ Coronation Market/ St. Mary (UWIM)

151 _____. "The Role and Status of Rural Jamaican Women: Higglering and Mothering." PhD thesis, University of California, Berkeley, 1976. 212 p.

Rural women/ Status/ Women's role/ Higglering/ Informal sector/ Motherhood/ Migration/ Households/ Family/ St. Mary/ Maroons (UWIM)

152 _____. *Women are Better Suited: Women in Industrial Development in the Caribbean*. 1984. 46 p.

Discusses the role of women workers in the industrial sector in the Caribbean. Field research was carried out in Jamaica as well as in other Caribbean territories.

Factory workers/ Industrial sector/ Sex discrimination/ Economic value of women's work (WB)

153 Edwards, Melvin R. *Jamaican Higglers: Their Significance and Potential*. Norwich: Geographical Abstracts for the Centre for Development Studies, University College, Swansea, 1980. 58 p.

Higglering/ Informal sector/ Marketing/ Social mobility/ Internal migration/ Migration (UWIM)

154 Elliot, Rita. "Women Working from Home." *Money Index*. No. 341 (1992): 24–27.

Work at home/ Home based business/ Women in business/ Entrepreneurs (UWIM)

155 "Freezone Woes." *Money Index*. No. 123 (1988): 14, 16.

Discusses the results of a survey of free zone workers.

Free zone workers/ Working conditions (UWIM)

156 Evering, Karlene. "Housing and Community Needs of the Aged in Salt Lane Community, Western Kingston, Jamaica." In *Learning about Women and Urban Services in Latin America and the Caribbean: a Report on the Women, Low Income Households and Urban Services Project of the Population Council*, edited by Marianne Schmink, Judith Bruce and Marilyn Kohn, p. 184–89. Washington, D.C.: Population Council, 1986.

Housing/ Older women/ Older men/ Living conditions/ Support systems/ Community (UDC)

157 Foner, Nancy. "Male and Female: Jamaican Migrants in London." *Anthropological Quarterly*. Vol. 49, no. 1 (1976): 28–33.

Migration/ Employment opportunities (UWIM)

158 French, Joan. "Defining Productive Women in Agriculture: the Case of Jamaica." In *Caribbean Women in Agriculture*, p. 77–85. Santiago, Chile: FAO, 1988.

Agriculture/ Rural women/ Farming statistics (UWIM)

159 _____, and Honor Ford-Smith. *Wid Dis Ring*. Toronto: Sister Vision, 1987. 35 p.

Based on research on women's work and organization in Jamaica, 1900–1944.

Working class women/ Comic books/ History/ Sistren Theatre Collective (UWIM)

160 _____. *Women, Work and Organization in Jamaica, 1900–1944*. Kingston: Sistren Theatre Collective, 1986. 396 leaves.

Women's organizations/ Women's rights/ Women's role/ Social movements (UWIM)

161 Galey, Sherry. *Guide to Selected Resources for Gender Sensitive Development Planning, Policy Formulation and Programme Implementation*. Kingston: Bureau of Women's Affairs, 1989. 50 p.

Women's role/ Development planning/ Income/ Education/ Development projects (ISER)

162 *Gender and Adjustment*. Prepared for the Office of Women in Development, Bureau for Program and Policy Coordination, US Agency for International Development by Mayatech Corporation. Silver Springs, MD: Mayatech Corporation, 1991. 194 p.

Study focuses on gender issues related to adjustment policies in developing countries. Case studies report situations in Jamaica, Ghana, Pakistan and the Ivory Coast.

Structural adjustment/ Education/ Labour force participation/ Income/ Nutrition/ Social conditions (UWIM)

163 Gillings, Scarlette. "Comparative Analysis of the Degree to Which Women Participate at all Levels in Decision Making Regarding Policies Concerning Health Services: Jamaican Study Paper." Prepared for the Multinational Study on Women as Providers of Health Care. Geneva, August 16–20, 1982. [62] p.

Health care workers/ Health planning/ Decision making (WB)

164 Girling, Robert, and Sherry Keith. "The Planning and Management of Jamaica's Special Employment Programme: Lessons and Limitations." *Social and Economic Studies*. Vol. 29, no. 2/3 (1980): 1–34.

Special Employment Programme/ Impact Programme/ Employment opportunities/ Government programmes (UWIM)

165 Gordon, Derek. "The Sexual Division of Labour and Intergenerational Mobility in Jamaica." In *Research in Social Stratification and Mobility*, edited by Robert V. Robinson, p. 215–38. Greenwich: Jai Press, 1987.

Social mobility/ Sexual division of labour/ Socioeconomic status (UWIM)

166 _____. "Women, Work and Social Mobility in Post-war Jamaica." In *Women and the Sexual Division of Labour in the Caribbean*, edited by Keith Hart, p. 67–80. Kingston: Consortium Graduate School of Social Sciences, 1989.

Labour force participation/ Social mobility/ Socioeconomic status/ Inequality (UWIM)

167 Gordon, Lorna. "Women in Caribbean Agriculture." In *Women in the Caribbean*, edited by Pat Ellis, p. 35–40. London: Zed Books, 1986.

Summarizes the findings of two surveys done on women in St. Lucia and Jamaica. Looks at the situation of rural families and rural women in farming, forestry and fishing.

Rural women/ Fishing/ Forestry/ Farmers/ Agriculture/ Rural families (UWIM)

168 Griffith, David C. "Women, Remittances and Reproduction." *American Ethnologist.* Vol. 12, no. 4 (1985): 676–90.

Examines the uses made by women of the money sent by men working in seasonal labour abroad.

Remittances/ Household income/ Family income/ Socioeconomic status/ Productivity (UWIM)

169 Hamilton, Marlene. "The Evidence of Sex-typed Behaviour in Professional Men and Women." *Sex Roles.* Vol. 11, no. 11/12 (1984): 1009–19.

Professionals/ Sex role stereotyping/ Attitudes (UWIM)

170 _____. "Sex Incongruous Occupational Roles." *Social and Economic Studies.* Vol. 34, no. 1 (1985): 97–111.

Sex role stereotyping/ Occupational roles/ Perception/ Adolescents (UWIM)

171 _____, and Elsa Leo-Rhynie. "Some Data on Professional Women in the Caribbean, with Particular Reference to Jamaica." *Concerning Women and Development.* Vol. 7 (1982). Barbados: WAND, 1982. 2 p.

Professionals/ Data analysis/ Careers/ Occupational roles (UWIM)

172 Harris-Williams, Sonia. "An Income Generating Project for Women in Rural Jamaica." In *Women of the Caribbean*, edited by Pat Ellis, p. 135–46. Kingston: Kingston Publishers, 1986.

Rural women/ Church projects/ Image of women/ Employment opportunities/ Handicraft/ Income generating projects/ Household income (UWIM)

173 _____. "The Second Integrated Rural Development Project (IRDP-II) of Jamaica: a Review of the Project Area Residents' Experiences and Responses to the Project." In *Planning for Women in Rural Development: a Source Book for the Caribbean*, p. 15–25. [Bridgetown]: Angela Zephririn Consultant Sales, 1983.

Rural women/ Agriculture/ Employment opportunities/ Integrated Rural Development Project (UWIM)

174 Harrison, Faye V. "Women in Jamaica's Urban Informal Economy: Insights from a Kingston Slum." *Nieuwe West-Indische Gids.* Vol. 62, nos. 3/4 (1988): 103–28.

Informal sector/ Inequality/ Exploitation/ Urban women (UWIM)

175 Henry-Wilson, Maxine. "Women and Career Development in Jamaica: a Review of Contemporary Research." Paper presented at the 13th Conference of the Caribbean Studies Association, Guadeloupe, 25–27 May 1988. 24 p.

Career development/ Labour force participation/ Sex role stereotyping (ISER)

176 *Higglering, Sidewalk Vending, Informal Commercial Trading in the Jamaican Economy: Proceedings of a Symposium May 21, 1988*, edited by Michael Witter. Kingston: University of the West Indies, Department of Economics, 1989. 76 p.

Informal sector/ Higglering/ Informal Commercial Importers (UWIM)

177 Katzin, Margaret Fisher. "The Business of Higglering in Jamaica." *Social and Economic Studies*. Vol. 9, no. 3 (1960): 297–331.

Higglering/ Informal sector/ Market vendors/ Rural women/ Informal savings (UWIM)

178 _____. "The Jamaica Country Higgler." *Social and Economic Studies*. Vol. 8, no. 4 (1959): 421–40.

Higglering/ Informal sector/ Market vendors/ Rural women (UWIM)

179 Kiaraing, Ilona. *Women and Non-traditional Vocational Training*. Kingston: HEART Trust, 1992. 20 p.

Job market/ Employment opportunities/ Vocational education/ Skills training/ Low income jobs/ Job discrimination/ Non-traditional occupations (ISER)

180 La Grenade, J. "Attitudes of Women Assuming Managerial Posts". Paper presented at Women as Providers of Health Care: Workshop held at the Social Welfare Training Centre, University of the West Indies, 16–19 July 1984. 5 p.

Executives/ Professionals/ Attitudes/ Health professionals (UWIM)

181 Le Franc, Elsie. "Petty Trading and Labour Mobility: Higglers in the Kingston Metropolitan Area." In *Women and the Sexual Division of Labour*, edited by Keith Hart, p. 99–132. Kingston: Consortium Graduate School of Social Sciences, University of the West Indies, 1989.

Higglering/ Informal sector/ Domestic trade/ Kingston/ Marketing / Socioeconomic status/ Social mobility/ Income (UWIM)

182 _____. "Small Hillside Farmers in Jamaica: a Social Analysis." Report submitted to the USAID Mission to Jamaica, 1986. 62 p.

Rural women/ Small farms/ Hillside farming/ Agriculture/ Socioeconomic status (ISER)

183 _____, Donna McFarlane, and Alicia Taylor. *The Informal Distribution Network in the Kingston Metropolitan Region.* Kingston: Institute of Social and Economic Research, University of the West Indies, 1985. 113 p.

Study examines nine categories of higglers, identifying levels of income and comparative economic status. Concludes that higglering is dominated by women and recommends that national development plans take account of skills acquired by higglers.

Informal sector/ Higglering/ Marketing/ Domestic trade/ Income/ Socioeconomic status/ Kingston (UWIM)

184 Leo-Rhynie, Elsa, and Marlene Hamilton. "Professional Jamaican Women – Equal or Not." *Caribbean Quarterly.* Vol. 29, no. 3/4 (1983): 70–85.

Professionals/ Sex discrimination/ Sex role stereotyping/ Job discrimination (UWIM)

185 Louat, Frederic, Margaret Grosh, and Jacques van der Gaag. *Welfare Implications of Female Headship in Jamaican Households.* Washington, D. C.: World Bank, 1993. 79 p.

Household composition/ Household income/ Child care/ Female headed households (UWIM)

186 Louden, Jonice. "Incorporating Women into Monitoring and Evaluation in Farming Systems Research and Extension." In *Gender Issues in Farming Systems Research and Extension*, edited by S.V. Poats, Marianne Schmink, and A. Spring, p. 87–97. Colorado: Westview Press, 1988.

Discusses the reasons for including gender issues in farming systems research and extension especially in Jamaica as women are actively involved in agricultural production.

Agricultural education/ Agricultural extension/ Small farms/ Agricultural information/ Farming systems/ Agriculture (MINAG)

187 Mair, Lucille Mathurin. "Jamaican Women and the Quest for Economic Independence." *Unesco Features*. No. 676/677/678 (1975): 11–14.

Status/ Exploitation/ Women's rights/ Economic value of women's work (UWIM)

188 Mason, Beverly J. "Jamaican Working Class Women: Producers and Reproducers." *Review of Black Political Economy*. Vol. 14, nos. 2–3 (1985–1986): 259–75.

Working class women/ Factory workers/ Productivity/ Socioeconomic status/ Household income/ Labour force participation/ Motherhood/ Women's role (UWIM)

189 McCaw, Affette. "Employment of Women in Health: Public and Private Sectors." Paper presented at Women as Providers of Health Care: Workshop held at the Social Welfare Training Centre, University of the West Indies, 16–19 July 1984. 16 p.

Health care workers/ Public sector employment/ Private sector employment (UWIM)

190 McFarlane, Glen. "A New Breed of Higgler Emerges in Jamaica." *Cajanus*. Vol. 17, no. 1 (1984): 5–7.

Higglering/ Informal sector (UWIM)

191 McFarquhar, E. L. "Constraints to Advancement of Women, Community, Family, Workplace and Changes Needed to Facilitate Advancement of Women." Paper presented at Women as Providers of Health Care: Workshop held at the Social Welfare Training Centre, University of the West Indies, July 16–19, 1984. 10 p.

Socioeconomic status/ Family/ Working conditions (UWIM)

192 McKay, Lesley. "Women's Contribution to Tourism in Negril, Jamaica." In *Women and Change in the Caribbean: a Pan Caribbean Perspective*, edited by Janet Momsen, p. 278–86. Kingston: Ian Randle Publishers, 1993.

Tourist industry/ Higglering/ Small business/ Boarding house owners/ Entrepreneurs (UWIM)

193 McLeod, Ruth. *The Women's Construction Collective: Building for the Future*. New York: Seeds, 1986. 24 p.

Skills training/ Construction industry/ Non-traditional occupations/ Women's Construction Collective/ Working class women/

Urban women/ Plumbing/ Masonary/ Carpentry/ Electrical installation/ Painting/ Steelwork (UWIM)

194 Meeks, Corina. "Women in the Public Information Services in Jamaica." In *Women and Media Decision Making in the Caribbean*, edited by Marlene Cuthbert, p. 121–33. Kingston: CARIMAC, University of the West Indies, 1982.

Agency for Public Information/ Women in the media/ Broadcasting industry (UWIM)

195 Mintz, Sidney W. "The Jamaican Internal Marketing Pattern: Some Notes and Hypotheses." *Social and Economic Studies*. Vol. 4, no. 1 (1955): 95–103.

Higglering/ Informal sector/ Marketing/ Agriculture (UWIM)

196 Munguia, Norma, Percy Aitken-Soux, Abdul Wahab, and Irving Johnson. *Salt Extraction by Solar Energy; a Mini Project: Rural Women Programme*. Kingston: IICA, 1980. 14 leaves.

Salt industry/ Rural women/ Development projects (MINAG)

197 _____, and Byron Lawrence. *Goat Revolving Scheme: a Project Model*. Kingston: Ministry of Agriculture and IICA Jamaica, 1980. 31 leaves.

Report of a joint programme carried out by the Ministry of Agriculture and Rural Women's Programme of the IICA Jamaica Office.

Goat rearing/ Agriculture/ Rural women/ Animal farming/ Development projects (MINAG)

198 National Development Foundation of Jamaica. Creative Energy Limited. *Report on the Training Needs Survey: Women in Small Business in Jamaica*. Kingston: NDF, 1990. 21 p.

Small business/ Entrepreneurs/ Training/ Socioeconomic status/ Training needs assessment (ISER)

199 *National Policy Statement on Women: Jamaica*. Kingston: Bureau of Women's Affairs, 1987. 5 p.

Women's participation/ Development planning/ Government policy/ National Policy Statement on Women (UWIM)

200 *National Report on the Status of Women in Jamaica.* Prepared for the Fourth World Conference on Women, Beijing, China, September, 1995. Kingston: Jamaica National Preparatory Commission, 1994. 118 p.

Women's participation/ Development planning/ Socioeconomic status/ Government policy (UWIM)

201 "Non-traditional Skills Training: the Kingston (Jamaica) Women's Construction Collective." In *Women, Technology and Microenterprise Development*, edited by Sarah E. Brayman, Marilyn Carr, and Charles Weiss, p. Ax-Axiii. New York: UNIFEM, 1991.

Women's Construction Collective/ Skills training/ Non-traditional occupations/ Working class women/ Vocational education/ Construction industry/ Carpentry (ISER)

202 Norton, A., and R. Symanski. "The Informal Marketing System in Jamaica." *Geographical Review.* Vol. 65, no. 4 (1975): 461–75.

Presents historical and geographical data on Jamaican agricultural practices and marketing systems and draws comparisons with Latin America. Some mention is made of women who, as later studies have shown, have traditionally controlled this sector.

Higglering/ Agricultural Marketing Corporation/ Agriculture/ Rural women/ Market vendors/ Informal sector (UWIM)

203 Norvell, Douglass, and Marian Kay Thompson. "Higglering and the Mystique of Pure Competition." *Social and Economic Studies.* Vol. 17, no. 4 (1968): 407–16.

Higglering/ Coronation Market/ Marketing/ Competition/ Informal sector/ Pricing (UWIM)

204 Pearson, Ruth. "Gender and New Technology in the Caribbean: New Work for Women." In *Women and Change in the Caribbean: a Pan-Caribbean Perspective*, edited by Janet Momsen, p. 287–95. Kingston: Ian Randle Publishers, 1993.

Data entry operators/ Technology/ Working class women (UWIM)

205 Pollock, Nancy J. "Women and the Division of Labor: a Jamaican Experience." *American Anthropologist.* Vol. 74, no. 3 (1972): 689–92.

Rural women/ Sexual division of labour/ Child care/ Subsistence farming/ Agriculture (UWIM)

206 Powell, Dorian. "Female Labour Force Participation and Fertility: an Exploratory Study of Jamaican Women." *Social and Economic Studies*. Vol. 25, no. 3 (1976): 234–58.
   Marriage/ Age/ Fertility/ Labour force participation/ Reproduction/ Union status (UWIM)

207 _____. "Occupational Choice and Role Conceptions of Nursing Students." *Social and Economic Studies*. Vol. 21, no. 3 (1972): 284–312.
   Student nurses/ Nursing schools/ Career choice/ Self-concept/ Nursing (UWIM)

208 _____. "Women, Work and the Family Project: Final Report." 1985. 192 p.
   Labour force participation/ Reproduction/ Child rearing/ Households/ Contraception/ Family (UWIM)

209 _____, and Tess Thomas. *Facts About Women*. Kingston: Soroptimist Club of Jamaica, 1975. 32 p.
   Statistics/ Education statistics/ Employment statistics (UWIM)

210 Repole, Dahlia. "Training Opportunities for Jamaican Women in Health Professions." Paper presented at Women as Providers of Health Care: Workshop held at the Social Welfare Training Centre, University of the West Indies, July 16–19, 1984. 49 p.
   Health care workers/ Training/ Continuing education (UWIM)

211 "Report of the Kelly Board of Enquiry into the Terms and Conditions of Employment in the Garment Industry: an Assessment," by the Women's Action Committee, prepared by Linnette Vassell, March 1990. 19 leaves.
   Free zone workers/ Garment industry/ Working conditions / Workers'rights/ Kingston Free Trade Zone (UWIM)

212 Ricketts, Mark. "The Woman as Investor." *Money Index*. No. 341 (1992): 3–5.
   Investment/ Money management/ Image of women (UWIM)

213 Seivwright, Mary J. "The Roles of Organisations of Women in Health Care." Paper presented at Women as Providers of Health Care: Workshop held at the Social Welfare Training Centre, University of the West Indies, July 16–19, 1984. 5 p.
  Heath care workers/ Women's organizations (UWIM)

214 Sinclair, Pat. *Development of a National Policy Statement: the Jamaican Experience*. Kingston: Bureau of Women's Affairs, 1987. 28 p.
  Women's participation/ Development planning/ Government policy/ National Policy Statement on Women

215 Smikle, C., and H. Taylor. *Higgler Survey: First Draft Report*. Kingston: Ministry of Agriculture, Agricultural Planning Unit, 1977. 105 leaves.
  Higglering/ Informal sector/ Markets/ Domestic trade (UWIM)

216 Standing, Guy. *Labour Commitment, Sexual Dualism and Industrialization in Jamaica*. Geneva: ILO, 1978. 23 leaves.
  Labour force participation/ Work attitude/ Work ethic/ Income/ Employment opportunities/ Labour supply (UWIM)

217 _____. *Unemployment and Female Labour: a Study of Labour Supply in Kingston, Jamaica*. New York: St. Martin's Press, 1981. 364 p.
  Labour supply/ Sexual division of labour/ Industrial sector/ Urban women/ Labour force participation (UWIM)

218 _____. "Female Labour Supply in an Urbanising Economy." In *Labour Force Participation in Low Income Countries*, edited by Guy Standing and Glen Sheehan, p. 87–122. Geneva: ILO, 1978.
  Labour supply/ Age/ Fertility/ Union status/ Socioeconomic status/ Income (UWIM)

219 *A Study on the Situation of Rural Families and Rural Women in Agriculture, Forestry and Fishery in Three Selected Areas in Jamaica: a Report to the FAO of the United Nations*. Kingston: Data Bank and Evaluation Division, Ministry of Agriculture, 1981. 1 v. (various pagings)
  Rural women/ Agriculture/ Forestry/ Fishery (MINAG)

220 Taylor, Alicia. *Characteristics of Male and Female-headed Households in Selected Areas of West Kingston – Salt Lane and Denham Town*. Kingston: Urban Development Corporation, 1983. 26 p.

Men/ Female headed households/ Income/ Salt Lane/ Denham Town/ Higglering/ Skills training/ Household size (UDC)

221 _____. "Women Traders in Jamaica: a Report on the Informal Commercial Importers." Commissioned by ECLAC. 1988. 27 p.
Informal sector/ Economic development/ Economic value of women's work/ Trade/ Informal Commercial Importers/ Entrepreneurs/ Vendors' Association/ Government policy/ Higglering (UDC)

222 Vassell, Linnette. "CUSO's Mandate on Women: Problems and Prospects in Jamaica." 1986. [49] p.
Local development agencies/ CUSO/ Development projects/ Women's organizations/ Women's participation (UWIM)

223 _____. "Jamaican Women in Business: Challenges and Visions." *Datapac: Caribbean Business Trends.* Vol. 10, no. 4 (1990): 13–27.
Entrepreneurs/ Female-male business relationships/ Women in business (PIOJ)

224 Webley, Beryl Joyce. "The Impact of the Nurse Practitioner on the Jamaica Health Care System." Master's thesis, University of the West Indies, 1990. 64 leaves.
Health care workers/ Health care services/Nurses (UWIM)

225 Westcarr, Eulie. "Factors Influencing the Migration of Jamaican Nurses." Master's thesis, University of the West Indies, 1990. 51 leaves.
Migration/ Nurses/ Brain drain/ Socioeconomic status/ Income (UWIM)

226 Wint, Adele J. *The Role of Women in the Development Process: Jamaica (with Special Reference to the Role of Rural Women).* Kingston: IICA, 1980. 76, 10 leaves.
Legislation/ Rural women/ Women's organizations/ Status/ Development/ Women's role (UWIM)

227 Wint, Eleanor Ann. *A Descriptive Study of Attitudes Towards Agricultural and Agro-industrial Pursuits Amongst Rural Women*, prepared for The Women's Bureau. Kingston: Women's Bureau, 1977. 37 p.
Rural women/ Agriculture/ Attitudes (WB)

228 "Women as Professionals." *Money Index*. No. 341 (1992): 36–40.
Professionals/ Executives (UWIM)

229 *Women as Providers of Health Care: Workshop Held at the Social Welfare Training Centre, University of the West Indies, July 16–19, 1984*. Kingston: Department of Social and Preventive Medicine, UWI, [1984]. 2 v.
Health care workers/ Health professionals/ Continuing education (UWIM)

230 "Women at the Workplace." Pts 1–2. *Investors Choice*. May and November (1992): 12 and 14–19.
Professionals/ Executives/ Women in business (UWIM)

231 "Women in Industry: Participatory Research Report on Garment Workers in Jamaica." Leith Dunn, research consultant. Summary prepared by Linette Vassell for the CUSO, May 1988. 16 leaves.
Free zone workers/ Garment industry/ Working conditions (UWIM)

232 "Women in Their Own Business." *Money Index*. No. 341 (1992): 29–35.
Women in business/ Entrepreneurs/ Women owned business (UWIM)

233 "Women Inc.: Dedicated to Improving Women's Lot." *Money Index*. No. 341 (1992): 41.
Women Inc/ Women's organizations/ Social services (UWIM)

Education 234-268

The earliest citation recorded here was published in 1835 dealing with destitute girls in Manchester. Other material encompasses the wide spectrum of formal and non-formal education and its impact on history, economics and sociology. Also included are studies related to adolescent girls, research dealing with sexism in textbooks and sex discrimination in education. The only material on science and technology identified relates to education and has been included in this section.

234 Adams, Daphne. "Vocational Training in Jamaica and the Opportunities for Female Participation." Caribbean Regional Seminar on Coordination of the Vocational Training of Women: Final Report. Port of Spain: ILO Caribbean Office, 1981.
    Vocational education/ Training/ Technical education/ Development projects/ Skills training

235 Bailey, Barbara. "Opportunities for Women in Non-formal Education: the Case of HEART." Paper Presented at the First Interdisciplinary Seminar on Women and Development Studies: Gender, Culture and Caribbean Development. Social Welfare Training Centre, UWI, Mona, June 8–19, 1987. 13 leaves.
    Vocational education/ Skills training/ HEART/ Adult education (UWIM)

236 Baxter, Ivy. "Women's Adult Education in Jamaica." [198–]. 12 leaves.
    Adult education (STC)

237 Carty, Linda. "Political Economy of Gender Inequality at the University of the West Indies." PhD thesis, University of Toronto, 1988. 294 leaves.

Suggests that women employed by the University of the West Indies are functioning in a male-dominated environment, which is a microcosm of the wider society. Finds that even with the increase in the numbers of women in higher education, not many are employed as faculty or as administrators. Discusses the attitudinal problems that exist between the different categories of women employees and concludes that the Women's Studies Group can be a catalyst for forging closer ties among these categories.

University of the West Indies/ Inequality/ Sex discrimination/ Job discrimination/ Attitudes/ Male dominance/ Professionals/ University workers/ Gender bias (ISER)

238 Craig, Christine. *I Can Be a ...: Guide to Skills Training Opportunities.* Kingston: Women's Bureau, 1978. 35 p.

Vocational education/ Skills training/ Adult education (WB)

239 Evans, Hyacinth. "Gender Socialization in Schools and Classrooms." Paper presented at the First Interdisciplinary Seminar on Women and Development Studies: Gender, Culture and Caribbean Development. Social Welfare Training Centre, UWI, Mona, June 8–19, 1987. 9 leaves.

Socialization/ Sex role stereotyping/ Teacher student interaction/ Adolescents/ Career choice (UWIM)

240 Female Refugee School. *Third Annual Report of the Female Refugee School at Fairfield, Manchester, Jamaica. Instituted October, 1832, under the patronage of the Countess Mulgrave.* October, 1835. Kingston: Printed at the Office of the Royal Gazette, 1835. 13 p.

Female Refugee School, Manchester/ Colonial education/ Destitute girls/ Girls (UWIM)

241 Hamilton, Marlene. "The Availability and Suitability of Educational Opportunities for Jamaican Female Students: an Historical Overview." Paper presented at the First Interdisciplinary Seminar on Women and Development Studies: Gender, Culture and Caribbean Development. Social Welfare Training Centre. UWI, Mona, June 8–19, 1987. 17 p.

Educational opportunities/ History (UWIM)

242 _____. "Gender Differences in Creativity: Fact or Fiction." Paper presented at the Third Disciplinary Seminar on Women and Development Studies: Gender and Education, Kingston, November, 1989. 12 leaves.

Text and data presented in this paper were taken from the article cited at no. 244. Author draws new conclusions and suggests additional explanations for her findings which partly support earlier views given.

Sex role stereotyping/ Adolescents/ Creativity/ Gender differences/ Performance (UWIM)

243 _____. "Performance Levels in Science and Other subjects for Jamaican Adolescents Attending Single-sex and Co-educational High Schools." *Science Education*. Vol. 64, no. 4 (1985): 535–47.

Adolescents/ Performance/ Academic achievement/ Science avoidance/ Secondary education/ Gender differences (UWIM)

244 _____. "Sex Difference in the Qualitative Performance of Jamaican Adolescents on the Circles Test of Creativity." *Caribbean Journal of Education*. Vol. 9, no. 2 (1982): 124–34.

Adolescents/ Gender differences/ Performance/ Creativity/ Sex role stereotyping (UWIM)

245 _____, and Elsa Leo-Rhynie. "Sex Role and Secondary Education in Jamaica." In *World Yearbook of Education, 1984: Women and Education*. London: Kogan Page, 1984. p. 123–38.

Sex role stereotyping/ Secondary education/ Adolescents (UWIM)

246 _____, and Elsa Leo-Rhynie. "Sex Role Stereotyping and Education: the Jamaican Perspective." *Interchange*. Vol. 10, no. 2 (1979–1980): 46–56.

Social norms/ Social roles/ Sex role stereotyping/ Secondary education (UWIM)

247 Harvey, Claudia, Vena Jules, Gwendoline Williams, Dianne Thurab, and Roslyn Carrington. *Gender Bias in Primary School Textbooks Used in Selected Commonwealth Caribbean Countries: an Exploratory Study*. London: Commonwealth Secretariat, 1990. 130 p.

Study analyses textbooks used in primary schools in Barbados, Guyana, Jamaica and St. Kitts-Nevis with a view to assessing gender bias.

Primary education/ Textbooks/ Gender bias/ Guyana/ Barbados/ St. Kitts Nevis (UWIM)

248 Howells, Carole A. "An Investigation of Personality Factors in Jamaican University Students." Master's thesis, University of the West Indies, 1978. 100 leaves.
Gender differences/ Personality/ University students (UWIM)

249 Jackson, Jennifer. "An Exploratory Study of Achievement Needs Among Girls Attending Secondary Schools in Jamaica." Master's thesis, University of the West Indies, 1979. 254 leaves.
Girls/ Secondary education/ Performance/ Home life/ Motivation/ Achievement need/ Academic achievement (UWIM)

250 Jackson, Trevor. "Women in Geology: a UWI Case Study." Paper presented at Third Disciplinary Seminar on Women and Development Studies: Gender and Education, Kingston, November, 1989. 10 leaves.
Geology/ Employment statistics/ University graduates/ Geologists/ Professionals (UWIM)

251 Leo-Rhynie, Elsa. "Educational Opportunities for Jamaican Female Students: a Contemporary Perspective." Paper presented at the First Interdisciplinary Seminar on Women and Development Studies: Gender, Culture and Caribbean Development, Kingston, 1987. 16 p.
Academic achievement/ Secondary education/ Adolescents/ Gender differences/ Performance/ Girls (UWIM)

252 _____. "Gender Issues in Education and Implications for Labour Force Participation." In *Women and the Sexual Division of Labour,* edited by Keith Hart, p. 81–97. Kingston: Consortium Graduate School of Social Sciences, University of the West Indies, 1989. Reprinted 1996.
Educational opportunities/ Career choice/ Labour supply/ Gender differences/ Sex role stereotyping/ Science avoidance/ Socialization (UWIM)

253 _____. "Gender Issues in Secondary School Placement." Paper presented at the Third Disciplinary Seminar on Women and Development Studies: Gender and Education, November 1989. 7 leaves.
Common Entrance Examinations/ Secondary education/ Secondary school placement/ Boys/ Girls/ Sex discrimination/ Gender bias (UWIM)

254 McKenzie, Hermione C. "Changing Female Educational Opportunities in Jamaica." Paper presented at IX World Congress of Sociology, Sociological Association, Uppsala, Sweden, August 1978.
Educational opportunities (STC)

255 McMillan, Veta. "Academic Motivation of Adolescent Jamaican Girls in Selected Single Sex and Co-educational Schools". Master's thesis, University of the West Indies, 1981. 91 leaves.
Academic achievement/ Secondary education/ Girls/ Sex role stereotyping/ Self-concept/ Life styles/ Home life/ Motivation (UWIM)

256 Miller, Errol. "Gender Composition of the Primary School Teaching Force: a Result of Personal Choice?" Paper presented at the Third Disciplinary Seminar on Women and Development Studies: Gender and Education, November 1989. 21 leaves.
Career choice/ Teachers/ Primary school teachers/ Female intensive occupations (UWIM)

257 _____. *The Marginalization of the Black Male: Insights from the Development of the Teaching Profession.* Kingston: Institute of Social and Economic Research, University of the West Indies, 1986. 88 p.
A second expanded and updated edition of this work has been published under the same title. Kingston: Canoe Press University of the West Indies, 1994. 135 p.
Men/ Teachers/ Career choice/ Female intensive occupations (UWIM)

258 _____. "Self-evaluation Among Jamaican High School Girls." *Social and Economic Studies.* Vol. 22, no. 4 (1973): 407–26.
Image of women/ Girls/ Colour/ Class/ Occupational roles/ Socioeconomic status/ Self-concept (UWIM)

259 _____. "A Study of Self-concept and its Relationship to Certain Physical, Social, Cognitive and Adjustment Variables in a Selected Group of Jamaican School Girls." PhD thesis, University of the West Indies, 1969. 324 leaves.
Self-concept/ Secondary education/ Physical appearance / Socioeconomic status/ Cognitive processes/ Girls/ Body image (UWIM)

260 Pencle, Carmen. "Student Perception of Women's Roles Now and in the Future." Master's thesis, University of the West Indies, 1994. 216 p.
   Sex role stereotyping/ High school students/ Attitudes/ Occupational roles (UWIM)

261 Pollard, Velma. "Images of Women in Some Modern Caribbean Texts." Paper presented at Third Disciplinary Seminar on Women and Development Studies: Gender and Education, November, 1988. 7 leaves.
   Olive Senior/ *Summer Lightning/ Arrival of the Snake Woman/* Image of women/ Role models/ Textbooks (UWIM)

262 Powell, Dorian. "The Professional Socialization of the Student Nurse: a Sociological Study of Two Schools of Nursing in Jamaica." Master's thesis, University of the West Indies, 1970. 197 leaves.
   Student nurses/ Professional development/ Training (UWIM)

263 Repole, Dahlia. "Alternative Futures: Intervention Initiatives." Paper presented at Third Disciplinary Seminar on Women and Development Studies: Gender and Education, November 1989. 28 p.
   Government policy/ Human resource development/ Empowerment/ Educational opportunities (UWIM)

264 Richardson, Mary. "An Identity Profile of Jamaican Students." Paper presented at Third Disciplinary Seminar on Women and Development Studies: Gender and Education, November 1989. 22 p.
   Identity/ Gender differences/ Self-concept/ Adolescents (UWIM)

265 Robotham, Hilary, and Yvette Jackson. "Women in Science and Technology in Jamaica." In *The Role of Women in the Development of Science and Technology in the Third World: Proceedings of the Conference Organised by the CIDA and the Third World Academy of Sciences.* edited by A. M. Fariqui, M. H. A. Hassan, and G. Sardn, p. 691–93. Singapore: World Scientific, 1991.
   Women in science/ Women in technology/ Women's role/ Science (UWIM)

266 Sahoy, Pauline. "Responding to Sexism in Education Through Text Analysis: Some Considerations." Paper presented at Third Disciplinary Seminar on Women and Development Studies: Gender and Education, November 1989, 42 leaves.

Sexism in education/ Textbooks/ Gender bias/ Sex discrimination (UWIM)

267 Salmon-Brouers, Elaine. "Information Needs of Science Teachers with Reference to the Role of Women in Science and Technology in Jamaica." In *The Role of Women in the Development of Science and Technology in the Third World: Proceedings of the Conference Organised by the CIDA and the Third World Academy of Sciences,* edited by A. M. Fariqui, M. H. A. Hassan and G. Sardn, p. 694–702. Singapore: World Scientific, 1991.

Science/ Technology/ Information resources/ Teachers/ Women's role/ Women in science/ Women in technology (UWIM)

268 Salter, Veronica. "Factors Affecting Females' Choice of Non-traditional Careers in Jamaica." Paper presented at Third Disciplinary Seminar on Women and Development Studies: Gender and Education, November 1989. 18 p.

Career choice/ Non-traditional occupations/ Socialization/ Educational opportunities (UWIM)

Family and Fertility 269-362

Early research on women dating back to 1955 is included in this section. These works support the view that such research was centered on the issue of fertility. Resources related to family planning, sexuality and sexual behaviour, family structure and family life are also listed.

269   Abdullah, Norma, and Susheila Singh. *Labour Force Participation and Fertility in Three Caribbean Countries*. St. Augustine, Trinidad and Tobago: UWI, ISER, 1984. 206 p.
      Labour supply/ Reproduction/ Sexual unions/ Contraception/ Labour force participation (UWIM)

270   Agyei, William K. A. "The Effects of Modernization on Fertility in Jamaica." PhD thesis, University of Maryland, 1976. 286 p.
      Migration/ Reproduction/ Mortality/ Urbanization/ Industrialization (UWIM)

271   Alexander, Jack. "The Role of the Male in the Middle Class Jamaican Family: a Comparative Perspective." *Journal of Comparative Family Studies*. Vol. 8, no. 3 (1977): 369–89.
      Middle class families/ Men/ Role expectation/ Family relationships/ Sex role stereotyping

272   Alleyne, Sylvan, Rosamund Rauseo D'Hereux, and Graham Serjeant. "Sexual Development and Fertility of Jamaican Female Patients with Homozygous Sickle Cell Disease." *Archives of Internal Medicine*. Vol 141, no. 10 (1981): 1295–97.

Sickle cell disease/ Pregnant women/ Sexual behaviour/ Union status/ Socioeconomic status (UWIM)

273 Anthony-Welch, Lillian. "A Comparative Analysis of the Black Woman as Transmitter of Black Values, Based on Case Studies of Families in Ghana and Among Jamaicans and Afro-Americans in Hartford Connecticut." EdD thesis, University of Massachusetts, 1976. 396 leaves.

African heritage/ Culture/ Motherhood/ Cultural heritage/ Social values (UWIM)

274 Back, Kurt W, and J. Mayone Stycos. *The Survey Under Unusual Conditions: the Jamaican Human Fertility Investigation.* Ithaca, New York: Society for Applied Anthropology, 1959. 52 p.

Reproduction/ Sexual behaviour/ Family planning (UWIM)

275 Bailey, Delfer M. "A Retrospective Study on the Psychological Effects Experienced by Women, 25–43 Age Who Had Voluntary (Female) Sterilization Done at Andrews Memorial Hospital and Glenn Vincent Poly Clinic, Kingston, Jamaica, 1991–1992." Master's thesis, University of the West Indies, 1993. 63 leaves.

Sterilization of women/ Birth control/ Psychological stress/ Psychosexual behaviour (UWIM)

276 Bailey, Wilma, Amy Lee, and Hugh Wynter. "Distance and Continuation Rates in a Family Planning Clinic: a Case Study From Jamaica." *Social and Economic Studies.* Vol. 36, no. 3 (1987): 203–17.

Looks at regular attendance at a family clinic by a group of acceptors of Depo Provera in relation to the distance between their homes and the clinic.

Birth control/ Family planning/ Contraception/ Contraceptive devices/ Family planning programmes/ Clinic attendance/ Depo Provera (UWIM)

277 _____, and Dorian Powell. "Patterns of Contraceptive Use in Kingston and St. Andrew 1970–1977." *Social Science and Medicine.* Vol. 16 (1982): 1675–83.

Contraception/ Contraceptive devices/ Sexual behaviour/ Birth control/ Family planning (UWIM)

278 _____, Hugh Wynter, and Amy Lee. "Women in Search of Stability." *Social Science and Medicine.* Vol. 26, no. 6 (1988): 619–23.

Contraception/ Union status/ Birth control/ Sterilization of women/ Sexual behaviour/ Female-male relationship/ Attitudes/ Family planning (UWIM)

279 _____, _____, _____, P. Oliver, and Jean Jackson, "The Effect of User Fees on the Utilization of Family Planning Services: a Clinical Study." *West Indian Medical Journal.* Vol 43, no. 2 (1994): 43–45.

Clinic attendance/ Family planning/ Costs/ Contraceptive devices/ Contraception/ Family planning programmes (UWIM)

280 Blake, Judith. "Family Instability and Reproductive Behaviours in Jamaica." In *Current Research in Human Fertility,* p. 24–41. New York: Milbank Memorial Fund. Current Research in Human Fertility: Papers Presented at the 1954 Annual Conference of the Milbank Memorial Fund.

Reproduction/ Family structure/ Union status (UWIM)

281 _____, J. Mayone Stycos, and Kingsley Davis. *Family Structure in Jamaica: the Social Context of Reproduction.* New York: Free Press, 1962. 262 p.

Family structure/ Union status/ Reproduction/ Marriage/ Contraception (UWIM)

282 Boland, Barbara Mary. "Union Status, Its Effects on Fertility and Mortality in Jamaica: Issues Re-examined." PhD thesis, University of Pennsylvania, 1983. 223 p.

Union status/ Mortality/ Contraception/ Socioeconomic status/ Culture/ Reproduction (UWIM)

283 Bracken, M. B. "Factors Associated with Dropping Out of Family Planning Clinics in Jamaica." *American Journal of Public Health.* Vol. 63, no. 3 (1973): 262–71.

Family planning programmes/ Clinic attendance/ Contraception (UWIM)

284 Brodber, Erna. "Family Structure and Sex Role Learning: a Study of Socialization in Jamaica." Master's thesis, University of the West Indies, 1968. 126 p.

Sex role stereotyping/ Family structure/ Socialization/ Child development (UWIM)

285 Brody, Eugene B. "Psychocultural Aspects of Contraceptive Behaviour in Jamaica." *Journal of Nervous and Mental Diseases.* Vol. 159, no. 2 (1974): 108–19.
Contraception/ Cultural heritage/ Cultural influences/ Belief systems (UWIM)

286 _____. *Sex, Contraception and Motherhood in Jamaica.* Cambridge, MA: Harvard University Press, 1981. 278 p.
Sexual behaviour/ Reproduction/ Child rearing/ Motherhood/ Contraception (UWIM)

287 _____, F. Ottey, and J. La Grenade. "Couple Communication in the Contraceptive Decision Making of Jamaican Women." *Journal of Nervous and Mental Disease.* Vol. 159, no. 6 (1974): 407–12.
Contraception/ Female-male relationship/ Sexual behaviour (UWIM)

288 _____, _____, _____. "Early Sex Education in Relationship to Later Coital and Reproductive Behaviour: Evidence from Jamaican Women." *American Journal of Psychiatry.* Vol. 133, no. 8 (1976): 969–72.
Sexual behaviour/ Contraception/ Sex education/ Reproduction (UWIM)

289 _____, _____, _____. "Fertility Related Behaviour in Jamaica." In *Cultural Factors and Population in Developing Countries,* p. 15–30. Washington, D. C.: Smithsonian Institution, 1976.
Reproduction/ Female-male relationship (UWIM)

290 Brown, Janet. *The Experience of Parenting: Brown's Hall.* Kingston: Regional Pre-School Child Development Centre, University of the West Indies, 1984. 34 p.
Parenting/ Child rearing/ Parent-child relationship (UWIM)

291 _____, Patricia Anderson, and Barry Chevannes. "Report on the Contribution of Caribbean Men to the Family: a Jamaican Pilot Study." Study funded by International Development Research Centre, Canada, UNICEF and CUSO, Jamaica, 1993. 203, [19] leaves.
Fathers/ Men/ Parent-child relationship/ Female-male relationship/ Parenting/ Child rearing/ Sexuality/ Sexual division of labour/ Domestic violence/ Income/ Education/ Birth control/ Contraception (UWIM)

292 Burrowes, J. T. "The Inter-uterine Contraceptive in Jamaica: a Preliminary Review." *West Indian Medical Journal.* Vol. 15, no. 1 (1966): 1–10.
Contraceptive devices/ Birth control/ Contraception (UWIM)

293 Carey-Lawrence, Beverly. "Farming, Family Life and Nutrition in Allsides, Trelawny: Six Case Studies." Master's thesis, University of the West Indies, 1981. 167 leaves.
Agriculture/ Rural women/ Nutrition/ Family structure/ Food (UWIM)

294 Chevannes, Barry. *Jamaican Men: Final Report to the National Family Planning Board on the In Depth Study of Jamaican Male Sexual Beliefs and Behaviour.* Kingston: The Board, 1985. 233 leaves.
Also published under the title: *Don't Be a Gladys.*
Sexual behaviour/ Men/ Sexuality/ Contraception (UWIM)

295 "Combining Career and Breast Feeding." *Cajanus.* Vol 12, no. 1 (1979): 13–16.
Breast feeding/ Working women/ Child care/ Motherhood (UWIM)

296 Cumper, George E. "The Fertility of Common-law Unions in Jamaica." *Social and Economic Studies.* Vol. 15, no. 3 (1966): 189–202.
Reproduction/ Birth rate/ Union status (UWIM)

297 Cunningham, W. E., and Winsome Segree. "Breast Feeding Promotion in an Urban and a Rural Hospital." *Social Science and Medicine.* Vol. 30, no. 3 (1990): 341–48.
Breast feeding/ Attitudes/ Child care (UWIM)

298 Davenport, William. "The Family System in Jamaica." *Social and Economic Studies.* Vol. 10. no. 4 (1961): 420–54.
Kinship/ Marriage/ Households/ Land tenure/ Union status/ Sexual behaviour/ Family structure (UWIM)

299 Denton, E. Hazel. "Economic Determinants of Fertility in Jamaica." *Population Studies.* Vol. 33, no. 2 (1979): 295–305.
Union status/ Socioeconomic status/ Motherhood/ Reproduction/ Working women/ Economic conditions (UWIM)

300 Dias, Patrick D. "Factors Affecting Age at Menarche and its Relationship to Other Indicators of Fertility of Teenage Females in the August Town Community, Jamaica." Master's thesis, University of the West Indies, 1986. 81 p.

Menstruation/ Sexual behaviour/ Girls/ Teenage pregnancy/ Nutrition (UWIM)

301 D'onofrio, Carol N., Donald H. Minkler, and Hamlet C. Pulley. *Evaluation of the Jamaican Family Planning Programme.* Washington, D.C.: American Public Health Association, 1974. 241 leaves.

Family planning programmes/ Contraception/ Birth control (UWIM)

302 Douglass, Lisa. *The Power of Sentiment: Love, Hierarchy and the Jamaican Family Elite.* Boulder, CO: Westview Press, 1992. 298 p.

Examines upper class families in Jamaica. Gives new insights into the colour/class hierarchy by considering how gender both affects what these categories represent and is itself a distinct dimension of the social order.

Elite/ Upper class families/ Kinship/ Social conditions/ Marriage/ Family structure (UWIM)

303 Ennew, Judith. "Family Structure, Unemployment and Child Labour in Jamaica." *Development and Change.* Vol. 13, no. 4 (1982): 551–63.

Child labour/ Survival strategies/ Household income/ Employment/ Family structure (UWIM)

304 *Family Life Education for All.* Kingston: Bureau of Health Education, 1974. 29 p.

Family life education (UWIM)

305 Farquharson, May. "A Short History of Family Planning in Jamaica." 1967. 2 p.

Birth control/ Family planning programmes (UWIM)

306 Grantham-McGregor, Sally, and E. H. Back. "Family Planning During the First Year after Delivery by Women in Kingston, Jamaica." *West Indian Medical Journal.* Vol. 21, no. 4 (1972): 249–52.

Birth control/ Contraception/ Family planning (UWIM)

307 _____, and Patricia Desai. "A Home Visiting Intervention Programme with Jamaican Mothers and Children." *Developmental Medicine and Child Neurology.* Vol. 17, no. 5, (1975): 605–13.

Home care services/ Motherhood/ Child rearing (UWIM)

308 Hall, Peter E. "The Introduction of Cyclofem into National Family Programmes: Experiences from Studies in Indonesia, Jamaica, Mexico, Thailand and Tunisia." *Contraception.* Vol. 49 (1994): 489–507.

Contraception/ Family planning/ Cyclofem (UWIM)

309 Hamilton, Pansy I. "Partner Support for Female Contraceptive Use." Master's thesis, University of the West Indies, 1989. 70 [43] leaves.

Birth control/ Female-male relationship/ Attitudes/ Sexual behaviour/ Contraception (UWIM)

310 Ibberson, D. "A Note on the Relationship Between Illegitimacy and the Birth Rate." *Social and Economic Studies.* Vol. 5, no. 1 (1956): 93–99.

Reproduction/ Birth rate/ Illegitimacy (UWIM)

311 International Statistical Institute. *The Jamaican Fertility Survey, 1975–76: a Summary of Findings.* Voorburg: International Institute, 1980. 13 p.

Jamaica Fertility Survey, 1975–76/ Demography/ Birth rate/ Union status/ Reproduction (UWIM)

312 Jack, Noreen Elizabeth. "A Comparison of a Jamaican Group of Teenage Mothers, and Teenage Girls Who Are Not Mothers, Regarding Selected Reproductive Issues." Master's thesis, University of the West Indies, 1988. 140 leaves.

Teenage mothers/ Attitudes/ Girls/ Sexual behaviour/ Reproduction (UWIM)

313 Jamaica. Department of Statistics. *Jamaica Fertility Survey 1975/ 76: Country Report.* Kingston: Department of Statistics, 1979. 2 v.

Jamaica Fertility Survey, 1975–76/ Demography/ Birth rate/ Union status/ Reproduction (UWIM)

314 Knight, Ronald. "A Knowledge, Attitude and Practice Study with Respect to Family Planning Among High School Students from

Barbados and Jamaica." Master's thesis, University of the West Indies, 1989. 97 leaves.

Sexual behaviour/ Birth control/ High school students/ Teenage pregnancy/ Attitudes/ Contraception (UWIM)

315 "Lactation, Fertility and the Working Woman." *Cajanus*. Vol. 10, no. 5 (1977): 260–66.

Breast feeding/ Working women/ Child care/ Motherhood (UWIM)

316 Lake, Obiagele. "A Feasibility Study on the Prevalence and Cultural Determinate of Breast Feeding Among Jamaica Rastafarians." MSc thesis, Cornell University, 1985. 186 leaves.

Rastafarian women/ Breast feeding/ Child care/ Nutrition/ African influences/ Motherhood (UWIM)

317 Landman, Jacqueline, Sally Grantham-McGregor, and Patricia Desai. "Child Rearing Practices in Kingston, Jamaica." *Caribbean Quarterly*. Vol. 29, nos. 3 and 4 (1983): 40–52.

Parenting/ Child rearing/ Working class women (UWIM)

318 _____, and V. Shaw-Lyon. "Breast Feeding Decline in Kingston, Jamaica, 1973." *West Indian Medical Journal*. Vol. 25, no. 1 (1976): 43–57.

Breast feeding/ Child care/ Attitudes/ Nutrition/ Motherhood (UWIM)

319 Le Franc, Elsie, M. Belinda Tucker, Gail Wyatt, Brendon Bain, and D. T. Simeon. "The Meaning of Sexual Partnerships: Re-examining the Jamaican Family System." *Bulletin of Eastern Caribbean Affairs*. Vol. 19, no. 4 (1994): 17–30.

Revisits the issue of union status and multiple partners. Identifies the lengths of unions and posits whether they eventually result in marriage. Concludes that serial rather than multiple partners, shorter relationships and decreasing numbers of marriages are now becoming the norm.

Union status/ Marriage/ Sexual behaviour (UWIM)

320 Leo-Rhynie, Elsa. *The Jamaican Family: Continuity and Change*. Kingston: Grace, Kennedy Foundation, 1993. 57 p.

Family structure/ Socialization/ Income/ Education/ Violence/ Parenting/ Value systems (UWIM)

321 Lightbourne, R. E., and Susheila Singh. "Fertility, Union Status and Partners in WFS Guyana and Jamaica Surveys, 1975–1976." *Population Studies.* Vol. 36, no. 2 (1982): 201–25.
Union status/ Birth rate/ Female-male relationship/ Reproduction/ Jamaica Fertility Surveys 1975–76 (UWIM)

322 MacCormack, Carol P. "Lay Concepts Affecting Utilization of Family Planning Services in Jamaica." *Journal of Tropical Medicine and Hygiene.* Vol. 88, no. 4 (1985): 281–85.
Contraception/ Attitudes/ Clinic attendance/ Fear (UWIM)

323 Mair, Lucille Mathurin. "Commentary on the Ethics of Induced Abortions from a Feminist Perspective." *International Journal of Gynaecology and Obstetrics.* Special Issue: Women's Health in the Third World. Supplement 3 (1989): 57–60.
Abortion rights/ Pro-choice/ Ethics/ Birth control (UWIM)

324 McFarlane, Carmen, and Charles Warren. *1989 Jamaica Contraceptive Prevalence Survey: Final Report.* Kingston: National Family Planning Board, 1990. 263 p.
Analyses data on contraceptive prevalence and discusses topics related to women and health. Some specific areas covered are fertility and the general factors that impact on fertility, infant and child mortality, maternal and child health and reproductive behaviour.
Contraception/ Health/ Child care/ Mortality/ Child health/ Birth control/ Reproduction/ Family planning programmes (UWIM)

325 _____, Jay S. Friedman, and Leo Morris. *Contraceptive Prevalence Survey, Jamaica 1993.* Kingston: National Family Planning Board, 1994. 5 v.
This study consists of five parts with the following titles: Administrative Report; Knowledge of and Attitudes Towards Family, Contraception and AIDS; Sexual Experience, Contraceptive Practice and Reproduction; Sexual Behaviour and Contraceptive Use Among Young Adults; Profiles of Health Regions. It seeks to update measures of fertility and contraceptive use among women, aged 15–44, young adults aged 15–24, and men aged 15–54. It provides information on the knowledge, attitudes and practices of contraception, the perceptions on the role of men and women on sexuality, child bearing, child rearing, health care and AIDS.
Contraception/ Health/ Child care/ Mortality/ Child health/ Birth

control/ Reproduction/ Family planning programmes/ AIDS/ Sexual behaviour (UWIM)

326 Morgan, B. I., and C. J. Stratmann. "The Jamaican Male and Family Planning." *West Indian Medical Journal.* Vol. 20 (1971): 5–11.
Men/ Contraception/ Sexual behaviour/ Family planning (UWIM)

327 National Family Planning Board. *Statistical Report, 1975.* Kingston: National Family Planning Board, 1975. 33 p.
Family planning programmes/ Contraception (UWIM)

328 Powell, Dorian. *Report on the Jamaica Contraceptive Prevalence Survey, 1983.* Kingston: National Family Planning Board, 1984. 171 p.
Birth control/ Child care/ Contraception/ Family planning programmes/ Reproduction (UWIM)

329 _____. "Sociological Aspects of Family Planning in Jamaica." 6 leaves.
Contraception/ Social conditions/ Family planning (UWIM)

330 _____, Linda Hewitt, and Prudence Woo Ming. *Contraceptive Use in Jamaica: the Social, Economic and Cultural Context.* Kingston: Institute of Social and Economic Research, University of the West Indies, 1978. 88 p.
Contraception/ Contraceptive devices/ Birth control/ Attitudes/ Cultural heritage (UWIM)

331 *Public Sector User Survey for Women 15–49 Years: Jamaica.* Kingston: Hope Enterprises, 1991. 1 v.
Profiles the user of public family planning services. Argues for some privatization of these services as findings establish that users are willing to pay if services are efficiently provided.
Family planning/ Family planning programmes/ Government policy/ Contraception/ Attitudes (ISER)

332 Rawlins, Joan. "Parent-child Interaction and Teenage Pregnancy: an Urban Study." Master's thesis, University of the West Indies, Mona, 1979. 130 leaves.
Parenting/ Teenage pregnancy/ Parent-child relationship (UWIM)

333 _____. "Parent Daughter Interaction and Teenage Pregnancy in Jamaica." *Journal of Comparative Family Studies.* Vol. 15, no. 1 (1984): 131–38.

Parenting/ Teenage pregnancy/ Parent-child relationship (UWIM)

334 _____. *Sexuality, Contraception and Family.* Paper Presented at the First Interdisciplinary Seminar on Women and Development Studies: Gender, Culture and Caribbean Development. Social Welfare Training Centre, UWI, Mona, June 8–19, 1987. 21 leaves.

Sexuality/ Contraception/ Female-male relationship/ Birth control/ Abortion/ Family life (UWIM)

335 *Report on the Caribbean Family Planning Conference, November 26–29, 1984, Jamaica Conference Centre.* Sponsored by the United Nations Fund for Population Activities and the National Family Planning Board. [Kingston: National Family Planning Board, 1985]. 96 p.

Family planning programmes/ Birth control/ Contraception (UWIM)

336 *Report on the National Conference on Fertility and the Adolescent.* Held at the Pegasus Hotel Jamaica, January 7–11, 1980. Kingston: Department of Sociology, University of the West Indies, 1980. 108 leaves.

Sexuality/ Birth control/ Contraception/ Adolescents (UWIM)

337 *Reproduction and Methods of Family Planning.* Kingston: Extra-Mural Department, University of the West Indies, 1975. 8 leaves.

Reproduction/ Birth control/ Contraception (UWIM)

338 Roberts, George. *Fertility and Mating in Four West Indian Populations: Trinidad and Tobago, Barbados, St. Vincent, Jamaica.* Kingston: Institute of Social and Economic Research, University of the West Indies, 1975. 341 p.

Birth rate/ Union status/ Socioeconomic status/ Education/ Age/ Reproduction/ Sterility (UWIM)

339 _____. "Some Aspects of Mating and Fertility in the West Indies." *Population Studies.* No. 8 (1955): 199–227.

Union status/ Reproduction/ Sexual behaviour/ Family structure (UWIM)

340 _____, and Sonja Sinclair. *Women in Jamaica: Patterns of Repro-duction and Family.* Millwood, New York: KTO Press, 1978. 346 p.

Sexual behaviour/ Child care/ Breast feeding/ Infant mortality / Marriage/ Family structure/ Menstruation/ Motherhood/ Reproduction (UWIM)

341 Sinclair, Sonja. "A Fertility Analysis of Jamaica: Recent Trends with Reference to the Parish of St. Ann." *Social and Economic Studies.* Vol. 23, no. 4 (1974): 588–635.

Contraception/ History/ Demography/ Reproduction/ Sterility/ Slavery/ Rural women (UWIM)

342 _____. "Socio-biological Perspectives of Female Reproduction in Jamaica." PhD thesis, University of Surrey, 1981. 410 p.

Reproduction/ Sexual behaviour/ Birth control/ Union status (UWIM)

343 Singh, Susheila. *Evaluation of the Jamaica Fertility Survey 1975–76.* London: World Fertility Survey, 1982. 51 p.

Reproduction/ Jamaica Fertility Survey 1975–76/ Union status/ Birth rate/ Age/ Mortality (UWIM)

344 _____. *Guyana, Jamaica and Trinidad: Socio-economic Differen-tials in Cumulative Fertility.* Voorburg: International Statistical Institute, 1984. 89 p.

Chapter 4 of this study: "Jamaica: Socioeconomic Differentials in Fertility" analyses the age of entry of participants into their first unions and other differentials such as residence, occupation and education, in order to explain the variance in fertility rates.

Socioeconomic status/ Union status/ Birth rate/ Occupations/ Education/ Reproduction (UWIM)

345 Smith, Karl A. "Current Research in Family Planning in Jamaica." *Milbank Memorial Fund Quarterly.* Vol. 46, no 3 (1965): 257–67.

Contraception/ Abortion/ Sexual behaviour/ Contraceptive devices / Family planning (UWIM)

346 _____. *Report on a Study of the Operations of the Kingston and St. Andrew Area Family Planning Clinics.* [Kingston: University of the West Indies, 1971]. 113 p.

Family planning programmes/ Contraception/ Counselling/ Health care workers (UWIM)

347 _____. "Some Socio-economic and Medical Problems Related to Family Planning in Jamaica." PhD thesis, Yale University, 1971. 376 p.

Family planning/ Contraception/ Clinic attendance/ Attitudes/ Rural women/ Sexual behaviour/ Socioeconomic status (UWIM)

348 _____, and Raymond Johnson. "Medical Opinion on Abortion in Jamaica: a National Delphi Survey of Physicians, Nurses and Midwives." *Studies in Family Planning.* Vol. 7, no. 12 (1976): 334–39.

Abortion/ Legalization/ Health care workers/ Medical ethics (UWIM)

349 Somerville, Trixie. "Family Planning and Education for Family Living in Jamaica." Presented at the Caribbean Health and Education Workshop, 19–26 November, 1973. Kingston: National Family Planning Board, 1973. 4 p.

Also published in the *Jamaican Nurse.* Vol. 14, no. 1 (1974): 20–22 under the title "The Family and Family Life Education."

Family life education/ Family planning (UWIM)

350 Stycos, J. Mayone. *The Control of Human Fertility in Jamaica.* Ithaca, New York: Cornell University Press, 1964. 377 p.

Family structure/ Union status/ Marriage/ Sexual behaviour/ Birth rate (UWIM)

351 _____. "Norms and Sexual Relations in Jamaica." In *Human Fertility in Latin America: Sociological Perspectives,* edited by Stycos J. Mayone, p. 187–201. Ithaca, New York: Cornell University Press, 1968.

Reproduction/ Sexual behaviour/ Union status/ Attitudes (UWIM)

352 _____, and Kurt W. Back. "Contraception and Catholicism in Jamaica." *Eugenics Quarterly.* Vol 5, no. 4 (1958): 216–20.

Contraception/ Religious sanctions/ Roman Catholic women

353 *Survey of Some Aspects of Family Planning in Rural Jamaica.* Kingston: Ministry of Agriculture, Data Bank and Evaluation Division, 1980. 71 p.

Rural women/ Men/ Attitudes/ Contraception/ Sexual behaviour (PIOJ)

354 Vadies, Eugene. *Assessment of the Logistics Associated with the Use of Depo Provera in Jamaica Through the National Family Planning Board.* Kingston: Pan American Health Organization, 1984. 15 p.

Contraception/ Birth control/ Depo Provera/ Contraceptive devices (UWIM)

355 Ward, Mavis Marva. "A Knowledge Attitude and Practice Study of High School and Secondary School Students with Regard to Contraception in Kingston and St. Andrew." Master's thesis, University of the West Indies, 1991. 67 leaves.

Contraception/ Adolescents/ Attitudes/ Sexual behaviour (UWIM)

356 Warren, Charles, Dorian Powell, Leo Morris, Jean Jackson, Pansy I. Hamilton. "Fertility and Family Planning Among Young Adults in Jamaica." *International Family Planning Perspectives.* Vol. 14, no. 4 (1988).

Adolescents/ Contraception/ Birth control/ Sexual behaviour

357 Whitehead, Tony L. "Men, Family and Family Planning: Male Role Perception and Performance in Jamaica Sugartown." PhD thesis, University of Pittsburg, 1976. 257 leaves.

Men/ Role expectation/ Contraception/ Birth control/ Attitudes (UWIM)

358 Williams, Alice B. "Effects of User Fees on the Utilization Pattern of Family Planning Services Care Centers in St. Elizabeth." Master's thesis, University of West Indies, 1994. 62 p.

Family planning/ St Elizabeth/ Costs/ Clinic attendance/ Contraception (UWIM)

359 Williams, Lillith. "Selected Environmental Variables Which Affect the Sexual Knowledge Beliefs and Practices of a Sample of Jamaican Adolescents." Master's thesis, University of the West Indies, 1992. 238 leaves.

Adolescents/ Attitudes/ Sexual behaviour/ Contraception/ Belief systems (UWIM)

360 Wint, Eleanor Ann. "The Consequences of Infertility: a Focus on Self-concept Measurement in Social Work Practice." PhD thesis, University of the West Indies, 1991. 312 leaves.

Infertility/ Self-concept/ Social work/ Attitudes (UWIM)

361 Wright, R. E. "Fertility, Partners and Female Labour Supply in Jamaica." *Genus.* Vol. 44, no. 3–4 (1988): 205–24.

Labour supply/ Jamaica Fertility Survey, 1975–1976/ Sexual behaviour/ Union status

362 Wynter, Hugh, L. Matadial, M. Harry, and G. Burkett. "Psychosexual Attitudes in the Female Following Sterilization." *International Surgery.* Vol 64, no. 5 (1979): 31–33.

Psychosexual behaviour/ Attitudes/ Sterilization of women/ Birth control (UWIM)

Health

This section includes material covering health care facilities available to women and female health disorders. Most of the material located focuses on pregnancy and the medical problems associated with it. The few items on nutrition, obesity, health problems of older women, occupational health hazards were welcome finds.

363 Ashley, Deanna, Affette McCaw-Binns, and Jean Golding. "Social Conditions and Health of Pregnant Jamaican Women." In *The Perinatal Mortality and Morbidity Study, Jamaica: Final Report*, p. 1–25. Kingston: University of the West Indies, 1989.

Socioeconomic status/ Pregnant women/ Nutrition/ Working women/ Union status/ Living standards (UWIM)

364 Ashmeade-Dyer, Alma E. M. "The Status of Maternal and Child Health Services for Jamaica, with Particular References to the Metropolitan Parishes of Kingston and St. Andrew." Diploma Public Health thesis, University of the West Indies, 1972. 94 leaves.

Health care services/ Maternal care/ Child care/ Urban women (UWIM)

365 Bain, Brendon, Pansy I. Hamilton, Hermi Hewitt, Dorothy King, and Pauline Johnson. *Fostering Collaboration Between Researchers and NGOs on Women and AIDS in Jamaica*. Kingston: UWICARE and ICRW, 1994. 28 p.

AIDS/ HIV/ Support systems/ Non governmental organizations (UWIM)

366 Bright, Winsome Rosemarie. "Serum Ferritin in Jamaica in Pregnant Women." Master's thesis, University of the West Indies, 1983. 189 leaves.
    Pregnant women/ Serum ferritin/ Iron deficiency (UWIM)

367 Broome, Dianne. "Aspects of Obesity in Suburban Kingston Women." Master's thesis, University of the West Indies, 1984. 149 leaves.
    Obesity/ Urban women/ Food consumption/ Exercise/ Body image/ Diseases/ Eating habits/ Nutrition (UWIM)

368 Bullard, Rhoda. "The Association of Social Economic and Other Variables with the Haemoglobin Level of Pregnant Women Attending two Antenatal Clinics in Kingston, 1990." Master's thesis, University of the West Indies, 1991. 99 leaves.
    Pregnant women/ Anemia/ Haemoglobin level/ Socioeconomic status/ Nutrition (UWIM)

369 Carter, Philaberta L. "An Epidemiological Study of Health Concerns of Imprisoned Women in Jamaica." Master's thesis, University of the West Indies, 1994. 71 leaves.
    Prisoners/ Fort Augusta Correctional Institution/ Health problems/ Diseases (UWIM)

370 Davidson, J. R. T. "Post-partum Mood Change in Jamaican Women: a Description and Discussion on its Significance." *British Journal of Psychiatry*. Vol. 121, no. 565 (1972): 659–63.
    Pregnant women/ Postpartum depression/ Socioeconomic status/ Depression (UWIM)

371 Dreher, Melanie, C. "Maternal-child Health and Ganga in Jamaica." In *Health Care in the Caribbean and Central America,* edited by Frank McGlynn, p. 55–67. Williamsburg, VA: College of William and Mary, 1984.
    Drug Abuse/ Child health/ Drug side effects (UWIM)

372 Eldemire, Denise. "An Epidemiological Survey of the Elderly in Jamaica." PhD thesis, University of the West Indies, 1993. 380 leaves.
    Older women/ Diseases/ Nutrition/ Health care services (UWIM)

373 Figueroa, J. P. "Breast Cancer in Perspective." *Jamaican Practitioner.* Vol. 10, no. 1 (1990): 5–6.
   Breast cancer (UWIM)

374 _____, Deanna Ashley, Affette McCaw-Binns. "An Evaluation of the Domiciliary Midwifery Services in Jamaica." *West Indian Medical Journal.* Vol. 39 (1990): 91–98.
   Midwifery/ Home birth/ Maternal care/ Health care services (UWIM)

375 French, Joan. "Women and Health: a Sistren Participatory Workshop." In *Gender in Caribbean Development: Papers Presented at the Inaugural Seminar of the University of the West Indies, Women and Development Project,* edited by Patricia Mohammed and Catherine Shepherd, p. 342–47. Kingston: UWI, The Project, 1988.
   Methodology/ Sistren Theatre Collective/ Women's participation/ Consciousness-raising/ Psychodrama (UWIM)

376 Gertler, Paul, Omar Rahman, Chris Feifer and Deanna Ashley. "Determinants of Pregnancy Outcomes and Targeting of Maternal Health Services in Jamaica." *Social Science and Medicine.* Vol. 37, no. 2 (1993): 199–211.
   Pregnant women/ Health care service/ Home birth/ Hospital deliveries (UWIM)

377 Golding, Jean, Deanna Ashley, Affette McCaw-Binns, J. W. Keeling, and T. Shenton. "Maternal Mortality in Jamaica: Socioeconomic factors." *Acta Obstetricia et Gynecologica Scandinavica,* Vol. 68 (1989): 581–87.
   Pregnant women/ Socioeconomic status/ Mortality (UWIM)

378 Grant, Mary L. "Knowledge Level Regarding Hypertension Among Female Clients Attending Primary Health Care Centres in Jamaica." *Cajanus.* Vol. 27, no. 2 (1994): 96–103.
   Hypertension/ Health education (UWIM)

379 Hall, John St. Elmo. "Plasma Zinc Levels Throughout Pregnancy: a Study in Jamaican Women, with Relevant Aspects of Nutrition." PhD thesis, University of Sheffield, 1985. 267 p.
   Pregnant women/ Nutrition/ Plasma zinc/ Blood disorders (UWIM)

380 Hayes, J. S., Melanie C. Dreher, and J. K. Nugent, "Newborn Outcomes with Maternal Marihuana Use in Jamaican Women." *Pediat-
ric Nursing*. Vol. 14, no. 2 (1988): 107–10.
   Drug abuse/ Infants/ Pregnant women/ Drug side effects/ Support systems (UWIM)

381 *Health and Nutrition of Women Engaged in Marketing Agricultural
Produce in Parochial Markets*. Kingston: Caribbean Food and Nu-
trition Institute, [1986?]. 66 p.
   Higglering/ Nutrition/ Health problems (UWIM)

382 "The Health Care System IV: Folk Healing in Eastern St. Thomas."
In Keith Alan vom Eigen, "Science and Spirit: Health Care Utiliza-
tion in Rural Jamaica." PhD thesis, Columbia University, 1992. p.
263–365.
   Discusses various folk healing styles practised in Jamaica. Of
particular relevance is the discussion of the work of Mother
Winslow and Mother Simpson two folk healers in St. Thomas.
   Folk healers/ Folk medicine/ St Thomas (UWIM)

383 Hopwood, Jennifer. "A Study of Gender Relationships and Their
Association With the Practice of Safe Sex by Women Who Call
into the National HIV/STD Helpline." Master's thesis, University
of the West Indies, 1994. 55 leaves.
   AIDS/ HIV/ Sexual behaviour/ Attitudes/ Sexually transmitted
diseases/ Support systems/ Health counselling/ Hotlines (UWIM)

384 Jelliffe, E. F. "Nutrition Education on the Maternity Ward or What
Mothers Believe They have Learned on the Maternity Ward." *West
Indian Medical Journal*. Vol. 20, no. 3 (1971): 177–83.
   Nutrition/ Pregnant women/ Health education (UWIM)

385 Johnson, Marcel P. "Knowledge Attitude and Practices of Women
Ages 18–44 years Regarding Obesity in Suburban Jamaica."
Master's thesis, University of the West Indies, 1991. 71 leaves.
   Obesity/ Attitudes/ Diets/ Eating habits/ Nutrition/ Urban
women (UWIM)

386 Jones, Stephen, D. A. Shickle, A. R. Goldstein, and Graham
Serjeant. "Acceptability of Antenatal Diagnosis for Sickle Cell Dis-
ease Among Jamaican Mothers and Female Patients." *West Indian
Medical Journal*. Vol 37, no. 1 (1988): 12–15.
   Sickle cell disease/ Pregnant women/ Abortion (UWIM)

387 Keeling, J. W, Affette McCaw-Binns, Deanna Ashley, and Jean
     Golding. "Maternal Mortality in Jamaica: Health Care Provision
     and Causes of Death." *International Journal of Gynaecology and
     Obstetrics.* Vol. 35 (1991): 19–27.
         The information on women gathered from this study has also
     been reported in J. W. Keeling, " Perinatal Mortality of Mothers
     and Children: the Jamaica Study." In *Birth Risks*, edited by David
     H. Baum p. 25–33. New York: Raven Press, 1993.
         Study conducted in 1986/7 to assess the details regarding the
     death of women during pregnancy. The findings indicate that the
     major factors contributing to mortality were hypertension,
     haemorrhage and infections.
         Health care services/ Pregnant women/ Mortality/ Hypertension
     (UWIM)

388 Landman, Jacqueline. "Anthropometry and Dietary Patterns of
     Pregnant Jamaicans." PhD thesis, University of the West Indies,
     1985. 551 leaves.
         Pregnant women/ Nutrition/ Socioeconomic status/ Folklore/
     Eating habits/ Pica/ Anthropometry/ Body image (UWIM)

389 _____, and John St Elmo Hall, "The Dietary Habits and Knowl-
     edge of Folklore of Pregnant Jamaican Women." *Ecology of Food
     and Nutrition.* Vol.12 (1983): 203–10.
         A study of 125 pregnant women shows evidence of a strong mix
     of traditional folklore with modern ideas. Most women reported
     changes in diet and cravings for certain types of food. Common
     among women of lower socioeconomic status were changes in diet
     associated with attempts to prevent malformations, birthmarks,
     foetal deaths and difficult deliveries.
         Pregnant women/ Diets/ Nutrition/ Eating habits/ Folklore /So-
     cioeconomic status (UWIM)

390 Mason, Carolyn. "Women as Mothers in Northern Ireland and Ja-
     maica; a Critique of the Transcultural Nursing Movement." *Inter-
     national Journal of Nursing.* Vol. 27, no. 4 (1990): 367–74.
         Motherhood/ Nursing/ Stereotypes (UWIM)

391 McCaw-Binns, Affette, M. Samms-Vaughan, and Deanna Ashley.
     "The Impact of Social and Biological Factors on Pregnancy Out-
     come in a Cohort of Jamaican Mothers." In *Perinatal Problems of
     Islands in Relation to the Prevention of Handicaps*, edited by C.
     Berchel [et al.], p. 52–64. France: Inserm, 1992.

Socioeconomic status/ Pregnant women/ Biological influences/
Physiology (UWIM)

392 McFarquhar, E. L. "Violence Against Women in Jamaica: a Public
Health Concern." Master's thesis, University of the West Indies,
1994. 63 [33] leaves.
   This thesis includes a list and description of organizations that
support abused and non-abused women.
   Violence against women/ Health care services/ Support systems/
Women's shelters/ Attitudes/ Women's organizations (UWIM)

393 Mesfin, Elizabeth, Dinesh P. Sinha, Peter J. Jutsum, William K.
Simmons, and Denise Eldemire. "Nutritional Status, Socioeco-
nomic Environment and Lifestyle of the Elderly in August Town,
Kingston, Jamaica." In *Midlife and Older Women in Latin America
and the Caribbean,* p. 211–26. Washington, D.C.: Pan American
Health Organization, 1989.
   August Town/ Older women/ Older men/ Socioeconomic status/
Households/ Life styles/ Health service utilization/ Nutrition/
Anthropometry/ Living conditions (UWIM)

394 Mohammed, Patricia. "Women and Health: a Sistren Participatory
Workshop, an Analysis of Method." *In Gender in Caribbean Devel-
opment: Papers Presented at the Inaugural Seminar of the Univer-
sity of the West Indies, Women and Development Project,* edited by
Patricia Mohammed and Catherine Shepherd, p. 348–52. Kingston:
The Project, 1988.
   Methodology/ Sistren Theatre Collective/ Women's participa-
tion/ Consciousness-raising/ Psychodrama (UWIM)

395 Morrow, Ardythe L. "Weight Gain in Pregnancy and Other Maternal Factors in Relation to Infant Birth Weight Among Jamaican
Women." Master's thesis, University of the West Indies, 1981. 125
leaves.
   Pregnant women/ Infants/ Weight/ Nutrition (UWIM)

396 Palmer Levy, Mervin N. "Changing Patterns in the Clinic Population and Utilization of the Antenatal Unit at the University Hospital
of the West Indies between 1980 and 1992." Master's thesis, University of the West Indies, 1994. 48 p.
   Health care services/ Pregnant women (UWIM)

397 *Perinatal Mortality in Jamaica. Paediatric and Perinatal Epidemi-ology.* Vol. 8 Supplement 1, April 1994, edited by T. J. Peters. Oxford: Blackwell Scientific, 1994. 188 p.

Pregnant women/ Lifestyles/ Socioeconomic status/ Mortality (UWIM)

398 Persaud, Vasil. "Cervical Cancer Detection in Jamaica: Cytologic Screening of a Sample Population." *International Journal of Gynaecology and Obstetrics.* Vol. 12, no. 4 (1974): 151–55.

Cervical cancer/ Working class women/ Socioeconomic status/ Sexual behaviour (UWIM)

399 Prabhakar, P., A. Bailey, Affette McCaw-Binns, and Deanna Ashley. "Seroprevalence of Toxoplasma Gondii, Rubella Virus, Cytomegalovirus, Herpes Simplex Virus (TORCH) and Syphilis in Jamaican Pregnant Woman." *West Indian Medical Journal.* Vol. 40 (1991): 166–69.

Sexually transmitted diseases/ Pregnant women/ Viral infections (UWIM)

400 _____, V. R. Narla, Parimi S. Prabhu, and Vasil Persaud. "Risk factors for Carcinoma of the Uterine Cervix in Jamaican Women." *West Indian Medical Journal.* Vol. 36, no. 2 (1987): 86–90.

Cervical cancer/ Risk factors/ Sexual behaviour (UWIM)

401 Ragoonanan, Selwyn F. "A Knowledge, Experience and Attitude Study of Menopause Among Public Health Nurses and Women Without Health Training in Jamaica and Trinidad and Tobago." Master's thesis, University of the West Indies, 1990. 74 p.

Menopause/ Public health nurses/ Nursing/ Counselling/ Attitudes/ Consciousness-raising (UWIM)

402 Rawlins, Joan, and Carol Sargent. *Factors Influencing Prenatal Care Use Among Low Income Jamaican Women.* Kingston: Institute of Social and Economic Research, University of the West Indies, 1989. 42 leaves. Also published: Washington, D.C.: International Centre for Research, 1990.

Seeks to identify the factors that cause some low income women to register for prenatal care later than the first trimester of pregnancy. Surveys 225 women attending the Victoria Jubilee Hospital and 50 in the May Pen and Cassava Piece Areas. Confirms that

16% of these women register in the first trimester and finds that a variety of reasons are responsible for this practice.

Working class women/ Prenatal care/ Maternal and infant welfare/ Health care services/ Pregnant women (UWIM)

403 Reid, Verna, and D. C. Garcia. "Use of Mammography in Jamaica: the Jamaica Cancer Society Experience." *West Indian Medical Journal.* Vol. 43, no. 2 (1994): 34–35.

Jamaica Cancer Society/ Mammography/ Disease prevention/ Breast cancer (UWIM)

404 Segree, Winsome. "Health Problems of Women in Jamaica." *Association of General Practitioners Newsletter.* Vol. 4, no. 2 (1984): 4–19.

Health problems/ Diseases (UWIM)

405 Singh, Praimanand M. B. "Relationship Between Health Problems Associated with Working in the Kingston Free Zone and Health Services Within the Free Zone." Master's thesis, University of the West Indies, 1990. 69 leaves.

Free zone workers/ Garment industry/ Health care services/ Working conditions/ Occupational health hazards (UWIM)

406 Smith, Ruperta. "Comparison of Diabetes Related Knowledge, Attitude and Practice Among Pregnant Diabetics at Corporate Area Public and Private Care Facilities, Jamaica." Master's thesis, University of the West Indies, 1994. 64 leaves.

Pregnant women/ Diabetes/ Health care services/ Attitudes/ Health education (UWIM)

407 Thomas, P., Deanna Ashley, G. W. Bernard. "Incidence, Risk Factors and Outcome of the Hypertensive Disorders of Pregnancy in Jamaica." *Clinical and Experimental Hypertension.* Vol. 9, Part B. (1990): 169–98.

Pregnant women/ Hypertension/ Diseases (UWIM)

408 Thomas, Shirley. "An Assessment of Maternity Services in Portland and St. Mary." Master's thesis, University of the West Indies, 1993. 117 leaves.

Pregnant women/ Health care services/ Portland/ St. Mary (UWIM)

409 Walker, G. J. A., Deanna Ashley, Affette McCaw-Binns, and G. W. Bernard. "Maternal Mortality in Jamaica." *Lancet*. No. 8479 (1986): 486–88.

Based on a survey carried out between 1981 and 1983 to identify causes of death during pregnancy in Jamaica. The main cause was identified as being related to hypertensive diseases.

Mortality/ Health problems/ Diseases/ Pregnant women/ Hypertension (UWIM)

410 _____, Affette McCaw-Binns, Deanna Ashley, and G. W. Bernard. "Identifying Maternal Deaths in Developing Countries: Experiences in Jamaica." *International Journal of Epidemiology*. Vol. 19, no. 3 (1990): 599–605.

The authors explore the theme of maternal mortality and suggest sources from which information can be obtained.

Pregnant women/ Mortality/ Medical records/ Information sources. (UWIM)

411 Walker, Susan, Sally Grantham-McGregor, John H. Hines, Sonia Williams, and Franklyn Bennett. *Nutrition of Adolescent Girls Research Programme*. Washington, D.C.: International Centre for Research on Women, 1994. 113 p.

Studies nutrition and health behaviour of adolescent girls. Concludes that nutritional status and health behaviour patterns affect school achievement, attendance and dropout levels.

Nutrition/ Girls/ Learning/ Academic achievement/ School attendance (UWIM)

412 Wedderburn, Maxine, and Mona Moore. *Qualitative Assessment of Attitudes Affecting Childbirth Choices of Jamaican Women*. Arlington, Virginia: MotherCare Project, 1990. 68 p.

Pregnant women/ Maternal care/ Child care/ Childbirth/ Home birth / Attitudes/ Hospital deliveries (UWIM)

413 Williams, Yasmin C. "Factors Governing the Contraction of Sexually Transmitted Disease in the Jamaican Woman." Master's thesis, University of the West Indies, 1992. 76 leaves.

Sexually transmitted diseases/ Sexual behaviour (UWIM)

History

Many of the works in this section can be described as having their groundings in Lucille Mair's seminal thesis of 1974. Various studies in the section document the experiences of women during the period of slavery and indentureship and the economic history of women's lives. Also identified are works that discuss the historical development of women's organizations which throw some light on social and political activism.

414 Bilby, Kenneth M., and Filomina C. Steady. "Black Women and Survival: a Maroon Case." In *Black Women Cross-culturally*, by Filomina C. Steady. Massachusetts: Schenkman, 1981. p. 451–67.
   Maroons/ Heroines/ Nanny/ Women of valour (UWIM)

415 Boa, Sheena Mary. "Free Black and Coloured Women in a White Man's Slave Society, Jamaica, 1760–1834." Master's thesis, University of the West Indies, 1985. 269 leaves.
   Freed women/ Socioeconomic status/ Educational opportunities/ Racism/ Sexual behaviour/ Sexual harassment (UWIM)

416 _____. "Freedwomen's Economic Contribution to Jamaica, 1760–1834." 8 p.
   Freed women/ Occupations/ Socioeconomic status/ Rural women/ Urban women/ Entrepreneurs (UWIM)

417 _____. "Urban Free Black and Coloured Women: Jamaica 1760–1834. *Jamaican Historical Review.* Vol. 18 (1993): 1–6.
   Freed women/ Occupations/ Middle class women/ Entrepreneurs/ Service occupations (UWIM)

418 Brathwaite, Edward Kamau. "Nanny, Palmares & the Caribbean Maroon Connexion." In *Maroon Heritage: Archaeological Ehnographic and Historical Perspectives,* edited by Kofi Agorsah, p. 119–38. Kingston: Canoe Press University of the West Indies, 1994.

Nanny/ Maroons/ Women of valour/ Leadership (UWIM)

419 _____. *Nanny, Sam Sharpe and the Struggle for People's Liberation.* Kingston: API, 1977. 64 p.

Heroines/ Nanny/ Maroons/ Sam Sharpe/ Churches/ Slave resistance/ Women of valour/ Leadership (UWIM)

420 _____. "Submerged Mothers." *Jamaica Journal.* Vol. 9, nos. 2–3 (1975): 48–49.

Herstory/ Slave resistance (UWIM)

421 Brodber, Erna. "Afro-Jamaican Women at the Turn of the Century." *Social and Economic Studies.* Vol. 35, no. 3 (1986): 23–46.

Female-male relationship/ Oral history/ Life stories (UWIM)

422 Bryan, Patrick. "Marriage and Family." In *The Jamaican People, 1880–1902,* by Patrick Bryan, p. 92–109. London: Macmillan, 1991.

An account of the professional women in Jamaican society during this period is given at p. 233–36.

Marriage/ Family/ Men/ Prostitution/ Sexual behaviour/ Professionals (UWIM)

423 Burnard, Trevor. "Inheritance and Independence, Women's Status in Early Colonial Jamaica." *William and Mary Quarterly.* Third series. Vol. 48, no. 1 (January 1991): 93–114.

Wills/ Inheritance/ Property ownership/ Socioeconomic status/ Widows/ Marital property (UWIM)

424 Cooper, Carolyn. " 'Resistance Science': Afrocentric Ideology in Vic Reid's *Nanny Town.*" In *Maroon Heritage: Archaeological Ethnographic and Historical Perspectives,* edited by Kofi Agorsah, p. 109–18. Kingston: Canoe Press University of the West Indies, 1994.

Nanny/ Maroons/ Slave resistance/ Victor Stafford Reid/ Nanny Town/ Protest action/ Women of valour (UWIM)

425 Dadzie, Stella. "Searching for the Invisible Woman, Slavery and Resistance in Jamaica." *Race & Class.* Vol. 32, no. 2 (1990): 21–38.

Slavery/ Historical analysis/ Cultural values/ Slave resistance (UWIM)

426 Ford-Smith, Honor. "Women and the Garvey Movement in Jamaica." In *Garvey: His Work and Impact,* edited by Rupert Lewis and Patrick Bryan, p. 73–83. Kingston: Institute of Social and Economic Research and the Department of Extra-Mural Studies, University of the West Indies, 1988.

Feminism/ UNIA/ Garvey Movement/ Image of women/ Leadership/ Black nationalism (UWIM)

427 French, Joan. *Colonial Policy Toward Women After the 1938 Uprising: the Case of Jamaica.* The Hague: Institute of Social Studies, 1988. 37 p.

Employment opportunities/ Development/ Colonial policy/ Government policy/ Socioeconomic status (UWIM)

428 Gayle, Dorette Ethline. "The Moravian Church and Women's Roles in Post Emancipation Jamaica, 1838–1865." Master's thesis, University of the West Indies, 1988. 103 leaves.

Church work/ Moravian Church/ Missionary work/ Church women (UWIM)

429 Higman, Barry. "Domestic Service in Jamaica Since 1750." In *Trade, Government and Society in Caribbean History, 1700–1920,* edited by Barry Higman, p. 117–38. Kingston: Heinemann, 1983.

Domestic workers/ Status/ Income/ Working conditions (UWIM)

430 _____. "Household Structure and Fertility on Jamaican Slave Plantations: a Nineteenth Century Example." *Population Studies.* Vol. 27, no. 2 (1973): 527–50.

Slavery/ Family structure/ Households/ Plantation society/ Birth rate (UWIM)

431 Hutton, Clinton Alexander. "The Suppression of the Black Woman." In Clinton Hutton, " 'Colour for Colour, Skin for Skin': the Ideological Foundations of Post-Slavery Society, 1838–1865: the Jamaica Case." PhD thesis, University of the West Indies, 1992. 431 leaves.

Women's role/ Occupations/ Female-male relationship/ Colonial policy/ Control/ Gender bias/ Subordination of women (UWIM)

432 Johnson, Michelle. "Domestic service in Jamaica: 1920–1970." Paper presented to Symposium on Caribbean Economic History, University of the West Indies, Mona, November 7–9, 1986. 39 p.

Domestic workers/ Urban migration/ Income/ Advertisements/ Working conditions (UWIM)

433 _____. "Intimate Enmity: Control of Women in Domestic Service in Jamaica, 1920–1970." *Jamaican Historical Review.* Vol. 18 (1993): 55–65.

Domestic workers/ Inequality/ Employment practices/ Living arrangements/ Worker employer relationship/ Advertisements/ Working conditions (UWIM)

434 Josephs, Aleric. "Gender and Occupations in Labour Force Statistics." Paper presented at the 25th Conference of the Association of Caribbean Historians, UWI, Mona, March 27–April 2, 1993. 26 p.

Labour supply/ Employment statistics/ Occupations/ Sexual division of labour (UWIM)

435 Kerr, Paulette. "Jamaican Female Lodging House Keepers in the Nineteenth Century." *Jamaican Historical Review.* Vol. 18 (1993): 7–17.

Occupations/ Boarding house owners/ Freed women/ Tavern keepers/ Entrepreneurs (UWIM)

436 Lobdell, Richard. "Women in the Jamaica Labour Force, 1881–1921." Paper presented to Symposium on Caribbean Economic History, University of the West Indies, Mona, November 7–9, 1986. 42 p.

Published in *Social and Economic Studies.* Vol. 37, nos. 1–2 (1988): 203–40.

Provides extensive statistical data on gender distribution in occupations in various parishes.

Labour supply/ Occupations/ Occupational patterns/ Agriculture/ Domestic workers/ Professionals/ Employment statistics (UWIM)

437 Mair, Lucille Mathurin. "A Historical Study of Women in Jamaica, 1655–1844." PhD thesis, University of the West Indies, 1974. 489 leaves.

Herstory/ Slave resistance/ Slavery/ Maroons (UWIM)

438 _____. "The Arrivals of Black Women." *Jamaica Journal.* Vol. 9, nos. 2–3 (1975): 2–7.

African heritage/ African societies/ Slavery/ Herstory (UWIM)

439 _____. *The Rebel Woman in the British West Indies During Slavery.* Kingston: Institute of Jamaica, 1975. 41 p.

African heritage/ Slave resistance/ Punishment/ Maroons/ Nanny/ Herstory/ Slavery/ Women of valour (UWIM)

440 _____. "Reluctant Matriarchs." *Savacou* 13 (1977): 1–6.

Image of women/ Plantation society/ Myths/ Status/ Stereotypes/ Herstory/ Slavery (UWIM)

441 _____. "Recollections of a Journey into the Rebel Past." In *Caribbean Women Writers: Essays from the First International Conference,* edited by Selwyn R. Cudjoe, p. 51–60. Wellesley, MA: Calaloux Publications, 1990.

Culture/ African heritage/ Herstory/ Slavery (UWIM)

442 _____. *Women Field Workers in Jamaica During Slavery.* Kingston: University of the West Indies, Department of History, 1987. 14 p.

Slavery/ Agriculture/ Labour supply/ Plantation society/ Herstory (UWIM)

443 Martin, Tony. "Women and the Garvey Movement." In *Garvey: His Work and Impact*, edited by Rupert Lewis and Patrick Bryan, p. 67–72. Kingston: Institute of Social and Economic Studies and the Department of Extra-Mural Studies, University of the West Indies, 1988.

UNIA/ Black nationalism/ Feminism/ Garvey Movement (UWIM)

444 Morrissey, Marietta. *Slave Women in the New World: Gender Stratification in the Caribbean.* Lawrence, KS: University of Kansas Press, 1989. 202 p.

Slavery/ Social classes/ Sex role stereotyping/ Social conditions/ Slave resistance/ Occupations/ Fertility/ Punishment/ Family/ Population ratio (UWIM)

445 Mullen, Michael. "Jamaican Maroon Women and the Cultural Dimension of American Negro Slavery." Paper presented at the 12th

Conference of the Association of Caribbean Historians, St Augustine, Trinidad and Tobago, March 29–April 4, 1980. 45 p.

Maroons/ Slavery/ Culture

446 Pigou-Dennis, Elizabeth. "Upper and Lower Class Women in Jamaica." Paper presented to the Social History Project 10th Anniversary Symposium, April 28, 1990, Department of History, University of the West Indies, Kingston. 20, [3] p.

Upper class women/ Working class women/ Women's roles/ Life styles/ Colonial society/ Social behaviour (UWIM)

447 Shepherd, Verene. "Indian Females in Jamaica; an Analysis of the Population Censuses, 1861–1943." *Jamaican Historical Review.* Vol. 18 (1993): 18–30.

East Indian women/ Female indentured workers/ Population distribution/ Occupations/ Social conditions/ Censuses (UWIM)

448 _____. "Indian Women in Jamaica, 1845–1945." In *Indenture and Exile: the Indo-Caribbean Experience,* edited by Frank Birbalsingh, p. 100–107. Toronto: Tsar Press, 1989.

East Indian women/ Female indentured workers (UWIM)

449 _____. *Transients to Settlers: the Experience of Indians in Jamaica, 1845–1940.* Leeds: Peepal Tree, 1994. 281 p.

Although this work examines Indian immigration in general there are pockets of information on women, particularly in the section on social customs and institutions where marriage, divorce and family life are discussed. Statistics on immigrant women are also provided.

East Indian women/ Female indentured workers (UWIM)

450 Simmonds, Lorna. "Higglers, Hucksters and Hirelings: Urban Female Slaves in the Internal Market System in Jamaica, 1780–1834." Paper Prepared for the Social History Workshop, University of the West Indies, Mona, November 1985. 26 p.

Higglering/ Urban female slaves/ Occupations/ Slavery/ Informal sector/ Marketing (UWIM)

451 _____. "Slave Higglering in Jamaica, 1780–1834." *Jamaica Journal.* Vol. 20, no. 1 (1987): 31–38.

Higglering/ Urban female slaves/ Slavery/ Marketing/ Legislation/ Informal sector (UWIM)

452 Teulon, Alan. "Nanny: Maroon Chieftainess." *Caribbean Quarterly*. Vol. 19, no. 4 (December 1973): 20–27.

Nanny/ Maroons/ Leadership/ Heroines/ Women of valour (UWIM)

453 Vassell, Linnette. "Accepting Ourselves to Change Ourselves: a Lesson of Testimonies by Women of the Jamaica Federation of Women." Paper presented to the Social History Project Tenth Anniversary Symposium, Department of History, UWI Mona, April 28, 1990. 14 leaves.

Jamaica Federation of Women/ Women's organizations/ Molly Huggins (UWIM)

454 _____. *Aspects of the Conditions of Jamaican Women in the Early 1940s*. Kingston: Department of History, University of the West Indies, 1987. 31 [3] p.

Socioeconomic status/ Income/ Employment/ Education (UWIM)

455 _____. "The Jamaican Federation of Women and Politics, 1944–1950." Paper presented at the 25th Conference of the Association of Caribbean Historians, UWI Mona, March 27–April 2, 1993. 31 p.

Feminism/ Leadership/ Women's rights/ Clubs/ Women's organizations/ Jamaica Federation of Women/ Molly Huggins/ Political activism (UWIM)

456 _____. "Voluntary Women's Associations in Jamaica: the Jamaica Federation of Women, 1944–1962." Master's thesis, University of the West Indies, 1993. 329 leaves.

Women's organizations/ Jamaica Federation of Women/ Molly Huggins/ Social work/ Social action (UWIM)

457 Warner-Lewis, Maureen. "The Nykuyu: Spirit Messengers of the Kumina." *Savacou* 13 (1977): 59–78.

Oral tradition/ Kumina/ African heritage/ Miss Queenie/ Ancestral spirits (UWIM)

458 Wilmot, Swithin. "Women and Protest in Jamaica, 1838–1865." Paper presented at the 19th Conference of the Association of Caribbean Historians, Fort-de-France, Martinique, April 13–17, 1987. 23 p.

Riots/ Protest action/ Socioeconomic status/ Freed women (UWIM)

Legal Issues and Laws

459–521

The LLB theses included in this section are housed at the Faculty of Law Library, University of the West Indies, Cave Hill, Barbados. Other material in the first part of this section centres generally on women's rights in the areas of marriage, property, family, support of children and employment. The second part lists various laws related to women's issues and the protection of women's rights.

Part 1: Secondary Sources

459 Agency for Public Information. *Know Your Rights: Maternity Leave With Pay.* Kingston: API, 1980. 5 p.
   Maternity leave/ Employee benefits (WB)

460 Alexander, Valerie. "The Family Court in Jamaica." LLB thesis, University of the West Indies, Cave Hill, 1976. 32 p.
   Family Court/ Family law/ Social services/ Family structure (UWIB)

461 Bennett, Kay V. "Marriage and Legitimacy: the Gap Between Law and Social Security in These Areas of Family Law in Jamaica." LLB thesis, University of the West Indies, Cave Hill, 1974. 34 p.
   Marriage law/ Illegitimacy/ Family law/ Family rights (UWIB)

462 Bennett, Lorna V. "The Legal Disabilities of Women." LLB thesis, University of the West Indies, Cave Hill, 1975. 47 p.
   Women's rights/ Equal opportunity (UWIB)

463 Boxhill, Eileen. "Developments in Family Law Since Emancipation." *West Indian Law Journal.* Special Issue (1985): 9–22.
Family law/ Family rights (UWIM)

464 _____. *Reforming the Law Relating to the Property Rights of Husband and Wife.* [Kingston: Law Reform Commission 197?]. 29 p.
Marital property/ Equitable distribution of marital property/ Women's rights/ Property ownership/ Marital property reform (WB)

465 _____. "Some Aspects of Family Law and Family Structure in Jamaica." LLB thesis, University of the West Indies, Cave Hill, 1973. 53 p.
Family law/ Family structure/ Family rights (UWIB)

466 Brady-Clarke, Cheryl. "The Matrimonial Causes Act 1989." *Caribbean Law Review.* Vol. 1, no. 1 (1991): 1–12.
Marriage law/ Women's rights (UWIM)

467 Bromfield, Holly. "The Rights of the Illegitimate Child under the Law in West Indian Society with Special Reference to Jamaica." LLB thesis, University of the West Indies, Cave Hill, 1974. 65 p.
Illegitimacy/ Family law/ Paternity/ Single mother's rights/ Women's rights (UWIB)

468 Craig, Christine. *Everything but the Ring.* From original research conducted by Margaret Forte. Kingston: Bureau of Women's Affairs, 1985. 34 p.
Union status/ Children/ Parenting/ Women's rights (WB)

469 Cumper, Gloria. *The Jamaican Woman and the Law: a Contribution to International Women's Year.* [Kingston]: Department of Statistics, [197?]. 6 p.
Women's rights/ Equal protection under the law (UWIM)

470 _____. *Planning and Implementing the Family Court Project, Jamaica.* Kingston: Institute of Social and Economic Research, University of the West Indies, 1981. 75 p.
Family law/ Family Court (UWIM)

471 _____. *Survey of Social Legislation in Jamaica.* Kingston: Institute of Social and Economic Research, University of the West Indies, 1972. 122 p.

Family law/ Social legislation/ Welfare reform/ Family rights (UWIM)

472 *The Family Law Committee Report on Matrimonial Property Law Reform.* Prepared by the JIS for the Ministry of Justice, Jamaica. Kingston: JIS, 1990. 21 p.

Marital property/ Equitable distribution of marital property/ Family law/ Women's rights/ Ownership (UWIM)

473 "Fort Augusta Women's Prison." In *Prison Conditions in Jamaica, May 1990: an Americas Watch Report.* p. 29–31. New York: Human Rights Watch, 1990.

Prisoners/ Fort Augusta Correctional Institution/ Prison conditions (UWIM)

474 Forte, Margaret. *Rights of Women in "Common Law" de Facto Unions in Jamaica.* [Kingston: Norman Manley Law School, 1982]. 46 p.

Women's rights/ Union status/ Equal protection under the law (WB)

475 Goldson, P. "Legalizing Abortion in Jamaica: Viewing Arguments For and Against Its Moral, Social and Medical Aspects." LLB thesis, University of the West Indies, Cave Hill, 1973. 41 p.

Abortion rights/ Ethics/ Pro-choice/ Medical ethics/ Social values/ Abortion laws (UWIB)

476 Jamaica. Department of Statistics. *Facts about Jamaican women.* Kingston: Department of Statistics, 1975. [12] p.

Women's rights (WB)

477 _____. Ministry of Health and Environmental Control. *Abortion: Statement and Policy by Minister of Health.* Kingston: The Ministry, 1975.

Abortion laws/ Government policy (WB)

478 _____. Ministry of Justice. Family Law Committee. *Divorce and Matrimonial Law: Interim Report.* Kingston: Government Printer, [1977?]. 22 p.

Divorce law/ Marriage law (WB)

479 _____. Ministry of Justice. Family Law Committee. *Working Paper on Matrimonial Property Reform*. Kingston: Family Law Committee, 1985. 27 p.

Equitable distribution of marital property/ Marital property reform/ Marital property (UWIM)

480 _____. Ministry of Social Security. *NIS Widow's Benefit*. [Kingston]: Ministry of Social Security, 1981. 1 folded leaf.

Insurance/ Widows/ Dependent benefits (WB)

481 Joint Trade Union Research Development Centre. *Focus on Women*. Kingston: JTURDC [1983]. 9 p.

Women's rights/ Equal protection under the law (WB)

482 Lawrence, Phoebe J. "A Critical Analysis of the Jamaica Maintenance Act." LLB thesis, University of the West Indies, Cave Hill, 1975. 96, 56 p.

Child support/ Maintenance Act/ Paternity/ Legal settlement (UWIB)

483 Miller, Carl. "The Relevance of the Law to the Concept of Family in the West Indies." LLB thesis, University of the West Indies, Cave Hill, 1973. 33 p.

Illegitimacy/ Family structure/ Family law (UWIB)

484 Muirhead, David. *Matrimonial Property Disputes Under the Married Women's Property Act*. [Kingston: s.n., 1978?]. 12 p.

Married Women's Property Act/ Equitable distribution of Marital property/ Marital property (WB)

485 Neita, Valerie. "The Sexual Offender: a Sociological Study of Sex Crimes in the Jamaican Society with a View to Reform the Laws and its Penal System." LLB thesis, University of the West Indies, Cave Hill, 1975. 72 p.

Sex crimes/ Violence against women/ Sentencing/ Legal reform/ Women's rights (UWIB)

486 Rickman, Millicent. "Women Workers and the Law: a Jamaican View." LLB thesis, University of the West Indies, Cave Hill, 1973. 50 p.

Labour law/ Equal opportunity/ Equal pay for equal work/ Sex discrimination/ Women's rights (UWIB)

487 Soroptimist Club of Jamaica. *Compilation and Analysis of Laws and Practices Discriminating Against Women in Jamaica.* Kingston: Soroptimist Club of Jamaica, 1975. 28 p.

Sex equity/ Women's rights/ Equal opportunity/ Equal protection under the law (WB)

488 Thompson, Marie E. "Family Planning in Jamaica: Some Legal and Sociological Implications." LLB thesis, University of the West Indies, 1983. 34, viii p.

Family planning programmes/ Social values (UWIB)

489 White, Paul A. "The Role of the Jamaican Father, Particularly the Father of the Illegitimate Child." LLB thesis, University of the West Indies, Cave Hill, 1975. 40 p.

Paternity/ Illegitimacy/ Fathers (UWIB)

490 Woodstock, Ena. "Law and the Status of Women in Jamaica." In *Law and the Status of Women: an International Symposium,* p. 165–83. New York: United Nations, Centre for Social Development and Humanitarian Affairs, 1977.

Status/ Women's rights/ Attitudes/ Equal opportunity

Part 2: Laws and Legislation

491 Divorce (War Marriages) Law, 1945. (Omitted from the 1973 Revised Edition of the Statutes but kept in force by the Law Revision Act).

492 Employment (Equal Pay for Men and Women) Act, 1975. Incorporated in 1973 Revised edition, 1976.

493 Hindu Marriage Act. (Part Omitted but kept in force 1973 by the Law Revision Act.)

494 Incest (Punishment) Act (1973 Revised Edition) with Amendment 1979.

495 Jamaica Nationality Act (1973 Revised Edition), with Amendments to 1983.

496 Judicature (Family Court) Act 1975. Revised Edition 1976 with Amendments to 1986.

497 Law Reform (Age of Majority) Act 1979. Revised Edition 1980.

498 Law Reform (Common Employment) Act. Revised Edition 1973.

499 Law Reform (Tort-Feasors) Act. Revised Edition 1973.

500 Legitimation Act. Revised Edition 1973.

501 Maintenance Act. Revised Edition 1973 with Amendments to 1987.

502 Maintenance Orders (Facilities for Enforcement) Act 1987.

503 Marriage Act. Revised Edition 1973 with Amendment 1979.

504 Marriage (Deceased Wife's Sister or Brother's Widow) Act. Revised Edition 1973.

505 Married Women's Property Act. Revised Edition 1973 with Amendments to 1978.

506 Maternity Leave Act 1979. Revised Edition 1980.

507 Matrimonial Causes Act 1989. Incorporated in 1973 Revised Edition (1990)

508 Minimum Wage Act. Revised Edition 1973 with Amendment 1974.

509 Muslim Marriage Act. Revised Edition 1973.

510 National Family Planning Act. Revised Edition 1973 with Amendment 1979.

511 National Heroes (Widows Pensions) Act 1974. Revised Edition 1975.

512 Nurses and Midwives Act. Revised Edition 1973.

513 Offences Against the Person Act. Revised Edition 1973 with Amendments to 1988.

514 Pensions Act. Revised Edition 1973 with Amendments to 1979.

515 Pensions (Civil Service Family Benefits) Act 1977. Revised Edition 1978.

516 Registration (Births and Deaths) Act. Revised Edition 1973 with Amendments to 1982.

517 Sex Disqualification (Removal) Law. Revised Edition 1953.

518 Solemnization of Marriages (Rev. Angus) (Validation etc.) Act 1975.

519 Status of Children Act 1976.

520 Wills Act. Revised Edition 1973 with Amendment 1979.

521 Women (Employment of) Act. Revised Edition 1973.

Politics

The common consensus is that women's involvement in politics in Jamaica is generally at the grassroots level and only a few advance to positions of leadership, authority and decision making. The paucity of material in this area reflects a growing need for comprehensive research on women's involvement in the political process. These few references, none of which are lengthy, point to the need for research on political activism, tenure in political office, voting patterns, resistance and political beliefs.

522 Edie, Carlene J. "Class, Gender and Party Leadership in the Caribbean: the Case of Jamaica." Paper presented at the 19th Conference of the Caribbean Studies Association, Mexico, May 1994. 33 p.

Analyses the leadership struggle in the People's National Party between Portia Simpson and P. J. Patterson in 1992. Discusses the issues of class, gender and education, which were important variables in the struggle. Suggests other factors that were also important, namely: the structure and organisation of the PNP, the perception of the declining role of charismatic leadership in Jamaica, and the importance of access to foreign governments and international lending agencies in maintaining the Jamaican political system.

Portia Simpson/ People's National Party/ Political participation/ Leadership

523 Gordon-Webley, Joan. "Problems Facing Women in Politics: Economics." In *Caribbean Women for Democracy*, edited by Marie Gregory p. 15–19. Kingston: Bustamante Institute of Public Affairs, 1985.

Political participation (UWIM)

524 Henry-Wilson, Maxine. "Women in Politics in Jamaica: Some Preliminary Findings." Paper presented at the Caribbean Studies Association Conference, Belize City, 1987. 42 p.

This paper is based on research carried out on women involved in representational politics at the local and national levels, senators, constituency caretakers and 23 women leaders of the women's arm of one political party. It discusses the experiences of the respondents during their period of activism, critical issues related to women's political participation and representation, policy issues, portfolio responsibilities and prospects for the future.

Political participation/ Political activism (UWIM)

525 _____. "Women's Participation in the Social and Political Process in Jamaica in the 1970s." 1986. 41 p.

Social action/ Political participation (UWIM)

526 Munroe, Ingrid. "Women's Emancipation: the Attitude and Practice of World Socialism and Our Party." In *Issues in Communist Rethinking, Workers Party of Jamaica.* 1987.

Workers Party of Jamaica/ Communism/ Socialism

527 People's National Party, Jamaica. *Human Resource Development: Harnessing People's Talents.* Kingston: PNP, 1987. 20 p.

Documents the Party's policy towards women on p. 10–12. Focuses on employment, legal reform, pregnancy among young girls, rural women, women in decision making and the media.

People's National Party/ Political party manifesto (UWIM)

528 _____. Women's Movement. Political Education Programme. *Lesson Guide to be Used in Meetings of the Women's Movement – 1980.* Kingston: PNP Women's Movement, 1980. 31 p.

People's National Party/ Political participation (UWIM)

529 Soares, Judith. "Women and Revolutionary Politics: the Case of the Workers Party of Jamaica." In *Forging Identities and Patterns of Development in Latin America and the Caribbean,* edited by Harry P. Diaz, Joanna W.A. Rummens, and Patrick D. M. Taylor, p. 157–67. Toronto: Canadian Scholars Press, 1991.

Workers Party of Jamaica/ Communism/ Socialism/ Radicalism (UWIM)

530 Vassell, Linnette. "The Movement for the Vote for Women." *Jamaican Historical Review.* Vol. 18 (1993): 40–54.

Voting rights/ Public opinion/ Women's rights/ Political activism/ Political participation/ Women's organizations (UWIM)

531 _____. "Women and Political Parties." Paper presented to WAND, Barbados, November, 1988. 10 leaves.

Organization of Women for Progress/ Political activism/ Women's organizations/ Women's rights/ Political participation (UWIM)

Social Conditions

Apart from material dealing with social conditions of women an eclectic array of subjects such as religion, aging, battered women, runaway mothers, lesbianism, sports and the subordination of women have been included here. All the subjects have social implications and are too sparse in number to be placed in separate categories.

532 Alexander, Jack. "Love, Race, Slavery and Sexuality in *Jamaican Images of the Family.*" In *Kinship, Ideology and Practice in Latin America*, edited by R. T. Smith, p. 147–80. Chapel Hill, NC: University of North Carolina, 1984.
   Slavery/ Sexuality/ Love/ Race/ Family (UWIM)

533 Allen, Elizabeth and Marcia Jones. *Role of the Bureau of Women's Affairs in the Implementation of the National Policy Statement on Women since 1987*. Kingston: Bureau of Women's Affairs, 1991. 49 p.
   Describes the structure, role and responsibilities of the Bureau. Assesses its effectiveness against the backdrop of the implementation of the National Policy Statement on Women, 1987.
   Women's rights/ Government policy/ Bureau of Women's Affairs/ National Policy Statement on Women, 1987 (UWIM)

534 Anderson, Beverley J. "Sports, Play, and Gender-based Success in Jamaica." *Arena Review*. Vol. 14, no. 1 (1990): 59–67.
   Seeks to develop a correlation between early socialization into sports as a determinant of occupational success. Concludes that in Jamaica this is not a variable and that other societal factors impinge on the advancement of women.
   Sports/ Socioeconomic status/ Achievement (UWIM)

535 Antrobus, Peggy. "Emerging Status of Jamaican Women." *Response: United Methodist Women.* Vol. 9, no. 6 (1977): 18–21.
Development planning/ Socioeconomic status/ Women's role (UWIM)

536 _____. "Government Programmes in Support of Women's Non-Productive Roles." Address to the Jamaica Federation of Women, March 14, 1977. 4 leaves.
Development planning/ Government policy (UWIM)

537 Bernal, Margaret, and Juliet Bruce. "Women and the Environment." In Consortium Alumni Association, *Caribbean Development: a Multi-Disciplinary Perspective,* p. 8–16. 1990.
Environment/ Environmental protection/ Sustainable development/ Women's role (ISER)

538 Besson, Jean. "Reputation and Respectability Reconsidered: a New Perspective on Afro-Caribbean Peasant Women." In *Women and Change in the Caribbean: a Pan-Caribbean Perspective,* edited by Janet Momsen, p. 15–39. Kingston: Ian Randle, 1993.
Peasantry/ Culture/ Role expectation/ Rural women/ Attitudes/ Social behaviour (UWIM)

539 Bolles, Augusta Lynn. "Goin' Abroad: Working Class Jamaican Women and Migration." In *Female Immigrants to the United States: Caribbean, Latin American and African Experiences,* edited by Delores M. Mortimer and Roy S. Bryce-Laporte, p. 56–84. Washington, D.C.: Research Institute on Immigration and Ethnic Studies, 1981.
Migration/ Socioeconomic status/ Working class women/ Employment opportunities (UWIM)

540 Boxill, Ian. *Perceptions of Gender Roles: Attitudes Toward Family Life and Sexual Behaviour in Urban Jamaica.* Kingston: University of the West Indies, Department of Sociology, 1994. 16 p.
Men/ Sex role stereotyping/ Sexual behaviour/ Female-male relationship/ Family (ISER)

541 Brodber, Erna. *Abandonment of Children in Jamaica.* Kingston: Institute of Social and Economic Research, University of the West Indies, 1974. 104 p.
Child care/ Parenting/ Runaway mothers/ Government policy/ Child welfare (UWIM)

542 _____. *Afro-Jamaican Women and Their Men in the Late Nine-teenth Century and First Half of the Twentieth Century.* Cave Hill, Barbados: Institute of Social and Economic Research, University of the West Indies, 1982. 39 p.

Life stories/ Men/ Social participation/ Rural communities/ Oral history/ Rural women/ Social behaviour (UWIM)

543 _____. *Perceptions of Caribbean Women: Towards a Documentation of Stereotypes.* Cave Hill, Barbados: Institute of Social and Economic Research, University of the West Indies, 1982. 62 p.

Attitudes/ Social behaviour/ Image of women/ Clergy/ Press/ Sex role stereotyping (UWIM)

544 _____. *Yards in the City of Kingston.* Kingston: Institute of Social and Economic Research, University of the West Indies, 1974. 87 p.

Residential units/ Yards/ Family/ Female-male relationship (UWIM)

545 Burke, Aggrey W. "Suicide in Jamaica." *West Indian Medical Journal.* Vol. 34, no. 1 (1985): 48–53.

Analyses seventy-six cases of sudden death in Jamaica during 1975–1976 to access possible cases of suicide deaths and the causes of these. Concludes that in the stable environment of a traditional society the clearly defined female role will act as a deterrent to suicide. The findings show that the rate of suicide of females was higher among the elderly and previously married, but lower among city dwellers.

Suicide/ Older women/ Women's role (UWIM)

546 Bryan, Beverley, Stella Dadzie, and Suzanne Scafe. *The Heart of the Race: Black Women's Lives in Britain.* London: Virago Press, 1986. 250 p.

Migration/ Racial discrimination/ Racism/ Socioeconomic status/ Health/ Education/ Self-concept (UWIM)

547 Chambers, Claudia, and Barry Chevannes. "Project: Sexual Decision-making Among Women and Men in Jamaica: Report on Six Focus Group Discussions." 1991. 26 p.

Men/ Sexual behaviour/ Sexuality/ Homosexuality/ Female-male relationship/ Violence against women/ Sexist language (ISER)

548 Chevannes, Barry. "Gender Ideology in Revivalism and Rastafari." Paper presented at the First Interdisciplinary Seminar on Women and Development Studies: Gender, Culture and Caribbean Development. Social Welfare Training Centre, UWI, Mona. June 8–19, 1987.

Rastafarian women/ Rastafarian Movement/ Revival Movement/ African heritage

549 _____. "Rastafari and Society." In Barry Chevannes, "Social and Ideological Origins of the Rastafari Movement in Jamaica," p. 399–425. PhD thesis, Columbia University, 1989.

Included in this chapter is a section on the changing roles of women in the Rastafarian movement.

Rastafarian women/ Rastafarian Movement (UWIM)

550 Clarke, Edith. *My Mother who Fathered me: a Study of the Family in Three Selected Communities of Jamaica.* 2d ed. London: Allen and Unwin, 1966. 227 p.

Social structure/ Female headed households/ Kinship/ Land tenure/ Marriage/ Sexual behaviour/ Family/ Socialization (UWIM)

551 Cuthbert, Marlene. *The Impact of Cultural Industries in the Field of Audio-visual Media on the Socio-cultural Behaviour of Women in Jamaica.* Paris: UNESCO, 1979. 47 p.

Study prepared for the meeting on the Impact of Cultural Industries in the Field of Audio Visual Media on the Socio-cultural Behaviour of Youth and Women held in Finland, 11–14 December, 1979. It looks at audiovisual media in Jamaica and the participation of Jamaican women in the global process of communication. It considers the representation and training of women professionals and makes recommendations for future policy.

Culture/ Communication/ Audiovisual media/ Women in the media (UWIM)

552 _____. "Woman Day a Come: Mass Media and Development in the Caribbean." *Media Development.* Vol. 31, no. 2 (1984): 18–21.

Looks at the image of women as portrayed in the press, radio, television and lyrics. Posits that the old stereotypes still prevail. Considers the entire Caribbean but draws on numerous examples of stereotyping that exist in all forms of Jamaican mass media.

Image of women/ Women in the media/ Media stereotyping/ Media portrayal/ Lyrics (UWIM)

553 De Veer, Henrietta. "Sex Roles and Social Stratification in Jamaica." PhD thesis, University of Chicago, 1979. 273 p.
Sex role stereotyping/ Social classes/ Women's role

554 Dixon, Mary. *New Dawn for Women.* Kingston: Jamal Foundation, 1975?, 31 p.
Women's rights/ Training/ Social mobility (UWIM)

555 Dreher, Melanie C. "Crack Use and Women in Jamaica." 1990. 85 p.
Analyses how women use cocaine. Identifies the psychological, social and economic paradigms that can assist in the establishment of preventative and treatment programmes.
Drug abuse/ Crack/ Cocaine/ Drug side effects/ Socioeconomic status/ Treatment programmes (ISER)

556 _____. "Marijuana Use Among Women: an Anthropological View." *Advances in Alcohol and Substance Abuse.* Vol. 3 (1984): 51–64.
Rural women/ Drug abuse (UWIM)

557 _____. "Poor and Pregnant: Perinatal Ganja Use in Rural Jamaica." *Advances in Alcohol and Substance Abuse.* Vol. 8, no. 1 (1989): 45–54.
Drug abuse/ Pregnant women/ Rural women (UWIM)

558 Ellis, Pat. *Women of the Caribbean.* Kingston: Kingston Publishers, 1986. 165 p.
History/ Culture/ Socioeconomic status/ Employment opportunities/ Educational opportunities/ Violence against women (UWIM)

559 Fisher, Michael M. J. "Value Assertation and Stratification: Religion and Marriage in Rural Jamaica." Parts 1 and 2. *Caribbean Studies.* Vol. 14, nos. 1 & 3 (1974): 5–37 & 7–35.
Marriage/ Religious beliefs/ Folklore/ Religion (UWIM)

560 Foner, Nancy. *Jamaica Farewell: Jamaican Migrants in London.* Berkeley, CA: UCLA Press, 1978. 262 p.
Chapter 3 of this work, " Women and Men" looks at the effects of gender on the migration patterns and experiences of migrants in London and at how migration changed the status of Jamaican migrant women.
Migration/ Gender differences/ Socioeconomic status/ Employment opportunities/ Family/ Sex role stereotyping/ London (UWIM)

561 _____. "Sex Roles and Sensibilities: Jamaican Women in New York and London." In *International Migration: the Female Experience*, edited by Rita James Simon and Caroline B. Brettell, p. 133–51. New Jersey: Rowman and Allanheld, 1986.

Migration/ New York City/ London/ Racial discrimination/ Sex discrimination/ Employment opportunities/ Sex role stereotyping (UWIM)

562 _____. "Women, Work and Migration: Jamaicans in London." *Urban Anthropology*. Vol. 4, no. 3 (1975): 229–49.

Also published in *New Community*. Vol. 5 no. 1–2 (1976): 85–98.

Migration/ Employment opportunities/ London/ Socioeconomic status/ Leisure (UWIM)

563 Ford-Smith, Honor. "Women's Place in Caribbean Social Change." In *Caribbean Reader on Development*, edited by Judith Wedderburn, p. 152–76. Kingston: Friedrich Ebert Stiftung, 1986.

Feminism/ History/ Women's organizations/ Social change/ Women's role/ Development (UWIM)

564 French, Joan. *No! to Sexual Violence*. Kingston: Sistren, 1985. 29 p.

Rape/ Sex crimes/ Violence against women/ Battered women (UWIM)

565 George, Vincent. *Housing for Elderly Women*. Kingston: National Housing Trust, 1991. 7, 5 p.

Housing/ Older women (ISER)

566 Gordon, Cynthia. "Interpersonal Relationships as a Source of Problems Experienced by Jamaican Adolescents." Master's thesis, University of the West Indies, 1983. 133 p.

Parent-child relationship/ Adolescents/ Communication/ Life styles/ Self-concept/ Parenting (UWIM)

567 Gordon, Derek. "Women and Class: Method and Substance." Paper presented at the Second Disciplinary Seminar on Women and Development Studies: Social Sciences, UWI, Cave Hill, Barbados, 3–7 April, 1989. 15 p.

Sociological analysis/ Social classes/ Social status/ Social mobility/ Men (UWIM)

568 Gordon, Lorna. "Silent Crimes Against Jamaican Women." In *Women of the Caribbean,* edited by Pat Ellis, p. 80–83. Kingston: Kingston Publishers, 1986.

Violence against women/ Abuse/ Battered women/ Sex crimes (UWIM)

569 Gordon, Shirley. *Ladies in Limbo: the Fate of Women's Bureaux: Six Case Studies from the Caribbean.* London: Commonwealth Secretariat, 1984. 126 p.

Case studies form the basis for a comparative discussion on the role of women's bureaux in Jamaica, Guyana, Barbados, Grenada, Dominica and Belize. The discussion focuses on the structure, staffing, objectives, responsibility and location of these offices and identifies common problems as well as achievements.

Government policy/ Bureau of Women's Affairs/ Services/ Development planning (UWIM)

570 Gregory, Carol. "Clergy Spouses and the Realities of the Manse." *Caribbean Journal of Religious Studies.* Vol. 10, no. 2 (1989): 66–80.

Church work/ Status/ Self-esteem/ Role expectations/ Self-concept (UWIM)

571 Hall, K. Ruth. *The Backyard Nursery: a Community Service in Hermitage and August Town: an Indigenous Approach to a Day Care Service for Children of Working Mothers.* Kingston: Department of Social and Preventive Medicine, University of the West Indies, 1976. 49 p.

Day care centres/ Child care/ Employment opportunities/ Older women (UWIM)

572 _____, Joan Rawlins, and A. K. Kumar, "Jamaica's Backyard Nurseries." *World Health Forum.* Vol. 5, no. 29 (1984): 136–37.

Day care centres/ Employment opportunities/ Older women/ Child care (UWIM)

573 Henry-Wilson, Maxine. "The Status of Jamaican Women, 1962 to the Present." In *Jamaica in Independence: Essays on the Early Years,* edited by Rex Nettleford, p. 229–53. London: James Currey; Kingston: Heinemann, 1989.

Socioeconomic status/ Labour supply/ Career choice/ Political participation/ Public administration/ Government policy (UWIM)

574 Jamaica Baptist Women's Federation. *Women's Federation 60th Anniversary, 1922–1982.* Kingston: JBWF, 1982. 24 p.

Women's organizations/ Jamaica Baptist Women's Federation/ Church work/ Social welfare (UWIM)

575 "Jamaican Women and Crack." *Network.* Vol. 1, no. 1 (1992): 1, 5.

Drug abuse/ Crack/ Drug side effects (PIOJ)

576 Keddie, A. M. "Psychosocial Factors Associated With Teenage Pregnancy in Jamaica." *Adolescence.* Vol 27, no. 108 (1992); 873–90.

Self-concept/ Teenage pregnancy/ Parenting/ Girls/ Psychological needs/ Father daughter relationships (UWIM)

577 Klak, Thomas H. and Jeanne K. Hey . "Gender and State Bias in Jamaican Housing Programs." *World Development.* Vol. 20, no. 2 (1992): 213–27.

Housing discrimination/ Sex discrimination/ Government policy/ Mortgages/ National Housing Trust/ Housing (UWIM)

578 Lake, Obiagele. "The Many Voices of Rastafarian Women: Sexual Subordination in the Midst of Liberation." *New West Indian Guide/ Nieuwe West-Indische Gids.* Vol. 68, nos. 3 & 4 (1994): 235–57.

Rastafarian women/ Female-male relationship/ Male dominance/ Subordination of women (UWIM)

579 MacCormack, Carol P., and Alizon Draper. "Social and Cognitive Aspects of Female Sexuality in Jamaica." In *Cultural Construction of Sexuality,* edited by Pat Caplan, p. 143–65. London: Tavistock, 1987.

Sexuality/ Identity/ Self-concept/ Attitudes/ Status (UWIM)

580 Mansingh, Akshai, and Paul Ramphal. "The Nature of Interpersonal Violence in Jamaica and its Strain on the National Health System." *West Indian Medical Journal.* Vol. 42, no. 2 (1993): 53–56.

Female-male relationships/ Female-female relationships/ Violence against women/ Health care services (UWIM)

581 McLeod, Ruth. *Daughters of Sysiphus: a Study of Gender-Related Behaviour in the Search for Shelter Among Low Income Heads of Households in Kingston, Jamaica.* Nairobi: UN Centre for Human Settlements, 1990. 149 p.

Housing/ Working class women/ Female headed households/ Socioeconomic status (UWIM)

582 McNeil, Pamela. *Programme for Adolescent Mothers: Projected Expansion and Provisional Future Plans.* Kingston: Women's Centre, 1985. 3 leaves.

Teenage mothers/ Welfare programmes/ Women's Centre (WB)

583 _____, Freya Olafson, Dorian Powell, and Jean Jackson. *The Adolescent Mother's Project in Jamaica.* Chestnut Hill, MA: Pathfinder Fund, 1980. 23 p.

Teenage mothers/ Welfare programmes/ Women's Centre (UWIM)

584 _____, Dorian Powell, Freya Olafson, and Jean Jackson. "The Women's Centre in Jamaica: an Innovative Project for Adolescent Mothers." *Studies in Family Planning.* Vol. 14, no. 5 (1983): 143–49.

Women's Centre/ Teenage mothers/ Welfare programmes (UWIM)

585 Meighoo, Kirk. "Violence Against Women: Policy Formulation and Conceptualization in Jamaica." 1994. 36 p.

Violence against women/ Government policy/ Women's rights (ISER)

586 Miller, Errol. "Body Image, Physical Beauty and Colour Among Jamaican Adolescents." *Social and Economic Studies.* Vol. 18, no. 1 (1969): 72–88.

Adolescents/ Body image/ Colour/ Beauty/ Urban youth/ Physical appearance/ Attitudes (UWIM)

587 _____. *Men at Risk.* Kingston: Jamaica Publishing House, 1991. 290 p.

Men/ Female-male relationship/ Sex discrimination/ Subordination of men (UWIM)

588 Mordecai, Martin. *Teenage Mother Project: Breaking the Cycle.* Kingston: Centre for Early Childhood Education, University of the West Indies, 1994. 20 p.

Teenage Mothers Project/Teenage mothers/ Parenting/ Sex education/ Skills training/ Counselling (UWIM)

589 Morrissey, Mike. *Women in Jamaica.* Kingston: Department of Statistics, 1975. 6 p.

Provides a brief analysis of statistics related to the distribution of women in the population based on the 1970 census report. Includes a map of Jamaica highlighting areas of distribution.

Population distribution/ Demography/ Female-male ratio (NLJ)

590 National Conference for International Women's Year. *Jamaican Women, a Plan for Action. Report.* Kingston: Women's Bureau, 1975. [98] leaves.

International Women's Year/ Women's rights/ Educational opportunities/ Employment opportunities/ Socioeconomic status/ Government policy (UWIM)

591 *National Symposium: Women and Development.* Co-ordinated by the Women's Bureau; sponsored by UNICEF, February 27, 1985, Bank of Jamaica Auditorium. Kingston: Women's Bureau, 1985. 111 leaves.

Women's participation/ Development planning/ Employment opportunities/ Health/ Educational opportunities/ Women in the media (WB)

592 Patterson, A.W. *Teenage Pregnancies: Their Implications for the Individual Family and Community.* Kingston: Bureau of Health Education, 1971. 8 leaves.

Family/ Teenage pregnancy/ Community (UWIM)

593 Powell, Dorian, and Jean Jackson. "Report of the Evaluation of the Women's Centre; Program for Pregnant Teenagers and Adolescent Mothers, Project of the Jamaican Women's Bureau." 1980. 99 leaves.

Women's Centre/ Teenage mothers/ Welfare programmes (WB)

594 _____, Jean Jackson, and Margaret Bernal. "Social Networks: a Resource Base for Urban Jamaican Women." Paper presented at the Women in the Caribbean Project Regional Conference, Barbados, September 12–16, 1982. 45 p.

Urban women/ Rural women/ Social networks/ Child care/ Kinship (UWIM)

595 _____, Jean Jackson, and Joanne Leslie. *Women's Work, Social Support Resources and Infant Feeding Practices in Jamaica.* Washington, D.C.: International Centre for Research on Women, 1988. 60 p.

Working women/ Child care/ Nutrition/ Weaning/ Breast feeding/ Growth/ Social networks/ Labour force participation/ Motherhood (UWIM)

596 Rawlins, Joan. "Middle Class Women in Jamaica: Life-cycle Events and Work." Paper presented at the Caribbean Studies Association Conference, Guadelope, May 25–27, 1988.
Middle class women/ Employment opportunities

597 _____. "Widowhood in Jamaica: Some Prelminary Findings." [Kingston: Institute of Social and Economic Research, University of the West Indies], 1987. 35 p.
Widows/ Socioeconomic status/ Older women/ Living conditions (UWIM)

598 _____. "Widowhood: the Social and Economic Consequences." In *Midlife and Older Women in Latin America and the Caribbean,* p. 323–30. Washington, D.C.: Pan American Health Organization, 1989.
Widows/ Socioeconomic status/ Older women/ Insurance/ Pensions / Living conditions/ Psychological stress (UWIM)

599 Reddock, Rhoda. "Feminism, Nationalism and the Early Women's Movement in the English-speaking Caribbean (with Special Reference to Jamaica and Trinidad and Tobago)." In *Caribbean Women Writers: Essays from the First International Conference,* edited by Selwyn R. Cudjoe, p. 51–60. Wellesley, MA: Calaloux Publications, 1990.
Feminism/ Women's organizations/ Nationalism/ Class struggle/ Trinidad and Tobago/ Women's role/ Lady Musgrave Self-help Society/ Jamaica Women's Social Service Club/ Coterie of Social Workers/ Clubs (UWIM)

600 "Report of the Jamaican Delegation to the 21st Assembly of the Inter-American Commission of Women." Prepared by the Bureau of Women's Affairs, 1982. 9 p.
Women's rights/ Socioeconomic status/ Sex equity (WB)

601 "Reports on the Status of Disabled Women in North America and Caribbean Region: Jamaica." In *Aim at the Sky: Report of the Disabled People's International Seminar, Roseau, Dominica, July 18–22, 1988,* p. 19–21. Kingston: DPI North America & Caribbean Regional Secretariat, 1989.

Disabled women/ Employment opportunities/ Family/ Self-concept / Public perception (UWIM)

602 Ross-Frankson, Joan. "The Economic Crisis and Prostitution in Jamaica: Preliminary Study." Paper presented at Issues Concerning Women: a Symposium Sponsored by the Department of Economics, University of the West Indies and Friedrich Ebert Stiftung, 7th March, 1987. 26 p.

This report is based on preliminary research carried out among "women hustlers" between mid 1985–December 1986. Twenty prostitutes between the ages of 16–43 years old were interviewed to find out the reasons they became prostitutes, the economic gains and the hazards of the trade.

Prostitution/ Socioeconomic status (UWIM)

603 Rowe, Audrey. "Preparation of Selected Jamaican Adolescents for Coping with Human Sexuality." Master's thesis, University of the West Indies, 1984. 204 leaves.

Adolescents/ Sexuality/ Sexual behaviour (UWIM)

604 Rowe, Maureen. "The Women in Rastafari." *Caribbean Quarterly.* Vol. 26, no. 4 (1980): 13–21.

Rastafari movement/ Role expectation/ Rastafarian women/ Women's role (UWIM)

605 Royale, Gloria. "Images of Women in Caribbean TV Ads: a Case Study." In *Women and Media Decision Making in the Caribbean,* edited by Marlene Cuthbert, p. 44–80. Kingston: CARIMAC, University of the West Indies, 1982.

Advertising/ Sex discrimination/ Media stereotyping/ Image of women/ Media portrayal (UWIM)

606 Senior, Olive. *Working Miracles: Women's Lives in the English-speaking Caribbean.* London: James Currey, 1991. 210 p.

Socialization/ Households/ Family/ Stereotypes/ Motherhood/ Working women/ Survival strategies/ Women's role/ Female-male relationship/ Women's organizations/ Political participation/ Socioeconomic status (UWIM)

607 Silvera, Makeda. "An Open Letter to Rastafarian Sisters: Dear Sisters." *Fireweed.* Vol. 16 (1983): 114–20.

Discusses the inequality faced by women in the Rastafarian movement.

Rastafarian women/ Equal rights/ Inequality (UWIM)

608 _____. "Man Royals and Sodomites: Some Thoughts on the Invisibility of Afro-Caribbean Lesbians." *Feminist Studies.* Vol. 18, no. 3 (1992): 521–32.

Discusses lesbianism in Jamaica and the secrecy surrounding the issue.

Lesbians/ Homosexuality/ Sexuality (UWIM)

609 *Situation Analysis of the Status of Children and Women in Jamaica.* Kingston: United Nations Children's Fund and Planning Institute of Jamaica, 1991. 148 p.

Child care/ Economic conditions/ Health/ Social services/ Funding agencies/ Education/ Development planning/ Health care services/ Socioeconomic status (UWIM)

610 Taylor, Janice D. "The Abuse of Women and Children in Jamaica." Prepared for the Women's Bureau in collaboration with Family Court and the Ministry of Justice. 1983. 45 p.

Child abuse/ Violence against women/ Battered women (WB)

611 Vendryes, Diane M. "Jamaican Working-class Women's Perception of Female Sex Role Attributes in Relationship to Ego Strength." Master's thesis, University of the West Indies, 1982. 96 p.

Working class women/ Sex role stereotyping/ Ego/ Self-concept/ Self-esteem (UWIM)

612 Watson, Ena May. "Coping Patterns Among Jamaican Households and Children's Creativity: a Study of Integrative Planning for Human Resource Development." PhD thesis, Case Western Reserve, 1976. 314 p.

Creativity/ Child rearing/ Households/ Parenting/ Family/ Socioeconomic status (UWIM)

613 White, Blossom Fay. "The Social and Psychological Contribution of Some Jamaican Low-income Males to Their Families." Master's thesis, University of the West Indies, 1992. 204 leaves.

Men/ Socialization/ Income/ Role expectation/ Socioeconomic status/ Female-male relationship/ Parenting/ Family responsibility/ Financial support

614 *Woman and Her Human Rights: a Programme for Progress.* Conference Sponsored by the Jamaican and Canadian National Commissions for UNESCO,, Kingston, Jamaica, 10–13 December, 1974. Conference report. Ottawa; Canadian Commission for UNESCO, 1975. 47 p.

Women's rights/ Development planning/ Socioeconomic status/ Employment opportunities/ Educational opportunities/ Legal rights (NLJ)

615 "Women and Philanthropy." In *Philanthropy and Social Welfare in Jamaica,* by Patrick Bryan, p. 34–41. Kingston: Institute of Social and Economic Research, University of the West Indies, 1990.

Women's organizations/ Social services/ Voluntary services/ Women's Self-help Society/ Upward and Onward Society/ Women's Social Services Association/ Jamaica Women's League/ Jamaica Women's Liberal Club/ Clubs/ Philanthropy (UWIM)

616 Yawney, Carole. "From Uncle Tom to Aunt Jemima: Towards a Global Perspective on Violence Against Women." *Canadian Woman Studies/Les Cahiers de la Femme.* Vol. 6, no. 1 (1985): 13–15.

Argues that the Rastafarian movement is a product of a patriarchal system and this legitimizes among other forms of oppression, violence against women.

Rastafarian women/ Violence against women/ Male dominance/ Subordination of women (UWIM)

617 _____. "Rastafarian Sister by the Rivers of Babylon." *Canadian Woman Studies/Les Cahiers de la Femme.* Vol. 5, no. 2 (1983): 73–75.

Brief assessment of the problems faced by women in the Rastafarian movement.

Rastafarian women/ Male dominance/ Subordination of women (UWIM)

618 _____. "To Grow a Daughter: Cultural Liberation and the Dynamics of Oppression in Jamaica." In *Feminism in Canada: from Pressure to Politics,* edited by Angela R. Miles and Geraldine Fine. p. 119–44. Montreal: Black Rose Books, 1983.

Rastafarian women/ Male dominance/ Culture/ Subordination of women (UWIM)

619 Cohen Stuart, Bertie A. *Women in the Caribbean: a Bibliography.* Lieden: Department of Caribbean Studies, Royal Institute of Linguistics and Anthropology, 1979–1985. 2 v.
   Caribbean Area/ Development/ Socioeconomic status (UWIM)

620 *Edna Manley Her Life and Work: a Selective Bibliography.* Kingston: National Library of Jamaica, [1984]. 4 leaves.
   Edna Manley/ Artists/ Sculptors (UWIM)

621 Instituto Interamericano de Ciencias Agrícolas. Committee for Rural Women and Development. *Rural Women: a Caribbean Bibliography with Special Reference to Jamaica.* San José, Costa Rica: IICA, 1980. 29 p.
   Lists 142 items arranged in three sections. Section A includes publications that the compiler feels are relevant to the study of women and development in general. Section B deals with rural women in Jamaica and Section C is a general list of material concerning women in Jamaica and the Caribbean.
   Rural women/ Agriculture/ Development/ Socioeconomic status/ Caribbean Area (UWIM)

622 Massiah, Jocelyn. *Women in the Caribbean: an Annotated Bibliography: a Guide to Material Available in Barbados.* Compiled with assistance of Audine Wilkinson and Norma Shorey. Cave Hill, Barbados: Institute of Social and Economic Studies (Eastern Caribbean), 1979. 133 p.

Development/ Socioeconomic status/ History/ Caribbean Area (UWIM)

623 McLean, Evadne. *Women and Development: a Selective Bibliography.* 1984, 24 p.

An annotated bibliography which covers material available at the Planning Institute of Jamaica and the ISER Documentation Centre, UWI (Mona). It is not limited to any geographical area and includes some items on Jamaica and the Caribbean.

Development/ Socioeconomic status/ Caribbean Area (UWIM)

624 Rawlins, Joan. *Family in the Caribbean, 1973–1986: an Annotated Bibliography.* Cave Hill, Barbados: Institute of Social and Economic Research, 1987. 41 p.

Marriage/ Family structure/ Social conditions/ Caribbean Area (UWIM)

Periodicals and Statistical Sources

Periodicals

625 *Adlib: the Voice of Women's Liberation in Jamaica.* (1973–). Kingston: Jamaica Women's Liberation Group (NLJ)

626 *Association of Women's Organizations in Jamaica: Newsletter.* Vol. 1, no. 1 (1989). Kingston: AWOJA (UWIM)

627 Bureau of Women's Affairs. *Annual Reports.* (1978–). Kingston: Bureau of Women's Affairs (WB)

628 *Family Planning News.* Vol. 1 (December 1972). Kingston: National Family Planning Board and the Jamaica Family Planning Association (UWIM)

629 Jamaica Family Planning Association. *Annual Reports.* (1966–). Kingston: Jamaica Family Planning Association (UWIM)

630 Jamaica Federation of Women. *Annual Reports* for the Years Ending March 31, 1952–1965. Kingston: Gleaner Co. (UWIM)

631 *Jamaican Nurse.* Vol. 1 (1961). Kingston: Nurses Association of Jamaica.
    Official publication of the Nurses Association of Jamaica. Normally includes articles on the history and development of the profession as well as biographical portraits of well-known Jamaican nurses (UWIM)

632 *Jamaica Pink Pages: Directory of Services of Women in Business.*
(1987–). Kingston: Educational and Administrative Management
Services (NLJ)

633 *Nanny: A Quarterly Newsletter of the Bureau of Women's Affairs,
Jamaica.* Vol. 1, no. 1 (May 1983). Kingston: Bureau of Women's
Affairs. Formerly published as *Women's Newsletter.* Vol. 1, no. 1,
Vol. 5 (1983) (UWIM)

634 *Sistren: A Quarterly Newsletter of Sistren Theatre Collective.* Vol.
1, no. 1 (1984). Kingston: The Collective.
Highlights issues concerning women in Jamaica as well as re-
porting on the work of Sistren Theatre Collective (UWIM)

635 Women and Development Studies (Mona). *Newsletter.* No. 1
(1988–1993). Kingston: Women and Development Studies Group
(Mona), University of the West Indies. Now called *Gender and Development Studies Newsletter.* (1993–) (UWIM)

636 *Women Can: Newsletter.* Vol. 1, no. 1 (1993). Kingston: Bureau of
Women's Affairs (WB)

637 *Women for Progress.* Vol. 1, no. 1 (1982). Kingston: Committee of
Women for Progress (UWIM)

Statistical Sources

The following citations provide statistical data on all aspects of Jamaican life. Particularly relevant here are sections giving statistical data on the economic and social conditions of women.

638 Planning Institute of Jamaica. *Economic and Social Survey, 1973–.* Kingston: Government Printer (UWIM)

639 *Population Census, 1991–.* Kingston: Statistical Institute of Jamaica, 1994. 1 v. in 14 parts.
    The most recent census data available on Jamaica. It provides statistical information under the following headings: age and sex; ethnic origin; religious affiliation; marital and union status; education; fertility; disability; economic activity; nationality; internal migration; housing (includes living conditions) (UWIM)

640 *Statistical Yearbook of Jamaica, 1973–.* Kingston: Department of Statistics (UWIM)

Audiovisual Material

641 *Jamaican Women.* [Videorecording]. New York: Martha Stuart Communications, 198? 3/4 U-matic, 29 mins.

Ten Jamaican women discuss marriage, their position in society, childbirth and what they consider to be the crucial years of their lives.

Marriage/ Socioeconomic status/ Reproduction/ Self-concept

642 *Miss Amy and Miss May.* [Videorecording]. Kingston: Sistren Theatre Collective, 1993. 40 mins.

Documents the life and work of Amy Bailey and May Farquharson.

Amy Bailey/ May Farquharson/ Social workers/ Teachers/ Social action (STC)

643 *Rastafari: Conversations Concerning Women.* [Videorecording]. [S.l.]: Eye and I Filmworks, 1983. 60 mins.

Interviews with Rastafarian men and women. Includes songs, chants, and poems and a discussion of taboos associated with women. Rastafarian women/ Subordination of women

644 *Sweet Sugar Rage: On Sistren's Popular Education Work With Female Sugar Workers.* [Videorecording]. Kingston: Sistren Theatre Collective, 1985. VHS or U-matic, 42 mins.

Agriculture/ Rural women/ Sugar workers (STC)

645 *Women Can.* [Videorecording]. Kingston: Bureau of Women's Affairs, 1993. 29 mins.

Highlights employment opportunities for women facilitated by the Bureau of Women's Affairs. Also focuses on a number of skill training programmes in non-traditional areas which are now available to women.

Skills training/ Employment opportunities/ Bureau of Women's Affairs (UWIM)

Appendix 1
Creative Writings

646–701

Literary Works of Women Authors for Whom
Critical Writings Appear in the Bibliography

646 Adisa Palmer, Opal. *Bake-face and Other Guava Stories*. Berkeley: Kelsey St. Press, 1987. 116 p.

647 _____. *Pina the Many-Eyed Fruit*. California: Julian Richardson, 1985. 26 p.

648 _____. *Tamarind and Mango Woman*: Poetry. Toronto: Sister Vision, 1991. 120 p.

649 _____, and Devorah Major. *Travelling Woman*. Oakland, Calif.: Jukebox Press, 1989.

650 Bennett, Louise. *Anancy and Miss Lou*. Kingston: Kingston Publishers, 1979. 82 p.

651 _____. *Anancy Stories and Poems in Dialect*. Kingston: Gleaner Company, 1944. 68 p.

652 _____. *Anancy Stories and Dialect Verse*. Kingston: Pioneer Press, 1957. 94 p.

653 _____. *Aunty Roachy Seh*. Edited by Mervyn Morris. Kingston: Sangsters, 1993. 171 p.

654 _____. (Jamaica) *Dialect Verse*. Kingston: Herald Ltd., 1942. 48 p.

655 _____. *Jamaica Labrish*. Kingston: Sangsters, 1966. 224 p.

656 _____. *Jamaica Maddah Goose*. Kingston: Friends of the Jamaica School of Art Association, 1981. 78 p.

657 _____. *Jamaican Dialect Poems*. Kingston: Gleaner Company, 1948. 185 p.

658 _____. *Selected Poems*. Edited with Introduction, Notes and Teaching Questions by Mervyn Morris. Kingston: Sangsters, 1982. 175 p.

659 Breeze, Jean. *Riddym Ravings and Other Poems*. London: Race Today Publications, 1988. 71 p.

660 _____. *Spring Cleaning*. London: Virago, 1992. 89 p.

661 Brodber, Erna. *Jane and Louisa Will Soon Come Home*. London: New Beacon, 1980. 147 p.

662 _____. *Louisiana*: a Novel. London: New Beacon, 1994. 166 p.

663 _____. *Myal*: a Novel. London: New Beacon, 1988. 111 p.

664 Campbell, Hazel. *The Rag Doll and Other Stories*. Kingston: Savacou, 1978. 56 p.

665 _____. *Singerman*. Leeds: Peepal Tree, 1992. 153 p.

666 _____. *Woman's Tongue*: Stories. Kingston: Savacou, 1985. 103 p.

667 Cliff, Michele. *Abeng*. New York: Penguin Books, 1984. 167 p.

668 _____. *Bodies of Water*. New York: Dutton, 1990. 155 p.

669 _____. *Claiming an Identity They Taught Me to Despise*. Watertown, Mass.: Persephone Press, 1980. 64 p.

670 _____. *Free Enterprise*. New York: Dutton, 1993. 213 p.

671 _____. *The Land of Look Behind*: Prose and Poetry. Ithaca, New York: Firebrand Books, 1985. 119 p.

672 _____. *No Telephone to Heaven*. London: Methuen, 1987. 211 p.

673 Cooper, Afua. *Breaking the Chains*. Toronto: Weelahs Publications, 1983. 48 p.

674 _____. *Memories Have Tongue*: Poetry. Toronto: Sister Vision, 1992. 107 p.

675 _____. *The Red Caterpillar on College Street*. Toronto: Sister Vision, 1989. 32 p.

676 Craig, Christine. *The Bird Gang*. Kingston: Heinemann, 1990. 56 p.

677 _____. *Mint Tea and Other Stories*. Oxford, Portsmouth: Heinemann, 1993. 150 p.

678 _____. *Quadrille for Tigers*. Berkeley, Calif.: Mina Press, 1984. 76 p.

679 D'Costa, Jean. *Escape to Last Man's Peak*. Kingston: Longman, 1975. 179 p.

680 _____. *Sprat Morrison*. Kingston: Ministry of Education, 1972. 189 p.

681 _____. *Voices in the Wind*. London: Longman, 1978. 147 p.

682 Goodison, Lorna. *Baby Mother and the King of Swords*. London: Longman, 1990. 84 p.

683 _____. *Heartease*. London: New Beacon, 1988. 61 p.

684 _____. *I Am Becoming My Mother*. London: New Beacon, 1986. 50 p.

685 _____. *Tamarind Season:* Poems. Kingston: Institute of Jamaica, 1980. 92 p.

686 Marson, Una. *Heights and Depths*: Poems. Kingston: Gleaner Company, 1931. 95 p.

687 _____. *The Moth and the Star*. Kingston: The Author, 1937. 103 p.

688 _____. *Towards the Stars*: Poems. Bickley, Kent: University of London, 1945. 63 p.

689 _____. *Tropic Reveries*: Poems. [S.I.: s.n., n.d.]. 88 p.

690 Riley, Joan. *A Kindness to the Children*. London: Women's Press, 1992. 312 p.

691 _____. *Romance*. London: Women's Press, 1988. 231 p.

692 _____. *The Unbelonging*. London: Women's Press, 1985. 144 p.

693 _____. *Waiting in the Twilight*. London: Women's Press, 1987. 165 p.

694 Senior, Olive. *Arrival of the Snake Woman and Other Stories*. London: Longman, 1989. 146 p.

695 _____. *Gardening in the Tropics*: Poems. Toronto: M&S, 1994. 136 p.

696 _____. *Summer Lightning and Other Stories*. London: Longman, 1986. 134 p.

697 _____. *Talking of Trees*. Kingston: Calabash, 1985. 86 p.

698 Thomas, Elean. *Before They Can Speak of Flowers*. London: Karia Press, 1988. 123 p.

699 _____. *The Last Room*. London: Virago, 1991. 200 p.

700 _____. *Word Rhythms From the Life of a Woman*. London: Karia Press, 1986. 112 p.

701 Wynter, Sylvia. *The Hills of Hebron*. London: Longman, 1984. 314 p.

Appendix 2
Author Index

Davidson, J. R. T., 370
Davies, Omar, 146
Davies, Rose, 147
Davis, Kingsley, 281
Dawes, Kwame (Neville), 27
De Veer, Henrietta, 553
Dewjee, Audrey, 79, 121
Denton, E. Hazel, 299
Desai, Patricia, 307, 317
Dias, Patrick D., 300
Dixon, Mary, 554
Douglass, Lisa, 302
Draper, Alizon, 579
Dreher, Melanie C., 371, 380, 555, 556, 557
Dunn, Leith, 149, 231
Dunn, Margaret, 56
Durant-Gonzalez, Victoria, 150, 151, 152

Ebanks, Roderick, 94
Edie, Carlene J., 522
Educational and Administrative Management Services, 632
Edwards, Melvin R., 153
Eldemire, Denise, 372, 393
Elliot, Rita, 154
Ellis, Pat, 558
Ennew, Judith, 303
Evans, Hyacinth, 239
Evering, Karlene, 156
Eye and I Filmworks, 643

Family Law Committee. *See* Jamaica. Ministry of Justice. Family Law Committee.
Farquharson, May, 305
Female Refugee School, Manchester 240
Feifer, Chris, 376

Fido, Elaine Savory, 28
Figueroa, J. P., 373, 374
Fisher, Michael M. J., 559
Foner, Nancy, 157, 560, 561, 562
Ford-Smith, Honor, 29, 30, 31, 32, 33, 34, 35, 36, 95, 123, 159, 160, 426, 563
Forte, Margaret, 474
Francis-Hinds, Suzanne, 37
Fraser, Lorna A., 38
French, Joan, 39, 158, 159, 160, 375, 427, 564
Friedman, Jay S., 325

Galey, Sherry, 161
Garcia, D. C., 403
Garvey, Amy Jacques, 96
Gayle, Dorette Ethline, 428
George, Vincent, 565
Gertler, Paul, 376
Gillings, Scarlette, 127, 163
Girling, Robert, 164
Gloudon, Barbara, 97, 98
Golding, Jean, 363, 377, 387
Goldson, P., 475
Goldstein, A. R., 386
Gonzalez, Anson, 40
Goodison, Lorna, 101, 682, 683, 684, 685
Gordon, Cynthia, 566
Gordon, Derek, 165, 166, 567
Gordon, Lorna, 167, 568
Gordon, Shirley, 569
Gordon-Gofton, Lorna. *See* Gordon, Lorna
Gordon-Webley, Joan, 523
Gradusov, Alex, 99
Grant, Mary L., 378
Grantham-McGregor, Sally, 306, 307, 317, 411

Katzin, Margaret Fisher, 177, 178
Keddie, A. M., 576
Keeling, J.W. 377, 387
Keith, Sherry, 164
Kelly Board of Enquiry, 211
Kerr, Paulette, 435
Kiaraing, Ilona, 179
King, Dorothy, 365
Klak, Thomas H., 577
Knight, Ronald, 314
Kumar, A. K., 572

La Granade, J., 180, 287, 288, 289
Lake, Obiagele, 316, 578
Landman, Jacqueline, 317, 318, 388, 389
Langley, W., 2
Lawrence, Byron, 197
Lawrence, Lebert, 127
Lawrence, Phoebe J., 482
Le Franc, Elsie, 181, 182, 183, 319
Lee, Amy, 276, 278, 279
Leo-Rhynie, Elsa, 171, 184, 245, 246, 251, 252, 253, 320
Leslie, Joanne, 595
Lewis, Martha W., 143
Lewis, Maureen Warner. *See* Warner Lewis, Maureen
Lewis, Rupert, 107
Liddell, Janice Lee, 50
Lightbourne, R. E., 321
Lobdell, Richard, 436
Louat, Frederic, 185
Louden, Jonice, 186
Lovindeer, Lloyd, 51

MacCormack, Carol P., 322, 579
MacLeavy, Jennifer Brown, 108
Mair, Lucille Mathurin, 187, 323, 437, 438, 439, 440, 441, 442

Major, Devorah, 649
Manley, Edna, 109
Manley, Rachel, 109
Mansingh, Akshai, 580
Marson, Una, 686, 687, 688, 689
Martha Stuart Communications, 641
Martin, Tony, 110, 443
Mason, Beverly J., 188
Mason, Carolyn, 390
Massiah, Jocelyn, 622
Matadial, L., 362
Mathurin Mair, Lucille. *See* Mair, Lucille Mathurin
Mayatech Corporation, 162
McCaffrey, Kathleen M., 52
McCaw-Binns, Affette, 189, 363, 374, 377, 387, 391, 399, 409, 410
McDonnough, Maxine, 111
McFarlane, B., 112
McFarlane, Carmen, 324, 325
McFarlane, Donna, 183
McFarlane, Glen, 190
McFarquhar, E. L., 191, 392
McIntosh, Sandy, 53
McKay, Lesley, 192
McKenzie, Hermoine C., 254
McLean, Evadne, 623
McLeod, Ruth, 193, 581
McMillan, Veta, 255
McNeil, Pamela, 582, 583, 584
Meeks, Corina, 194
Meighoo, Kirk, 585
Mesfin, Elizabeth, 393
Miller, Carl, 483
Miller, Errol, 256, 257, 258, 259, 586, 587
Minkler, Donald H., 301
Mintz, Sidney W., 195
Mohammed, Patricia, 394
Moore, Mona, 412

Appendix 3
Subject Index

Biological influences, 391
Birth control. *See* Contraception
Black nationalism, 88, 95, 107, 110, 111, 124, 426, 443
Boarding house owners, 192, 435
Body image, 259, 367, 388, 586
Breast cancer, 373, 403
Breast feeding, 295, 297, 315, 316, 318, 340, 595
Breeze, Jean, 18, 23, 77, 78, 82
Brodber, Erna, 3, 10, 12, 13, 14, 22, 26, 38, 46, 48, 54, 62, 64, 83, 115
Brown, Rosemary, 85
Bureau of Women's Affairs, 129, 130, 132, 533, 569, 645
Bustamante, Gladys, 97

Campbell, Hazel, 63
Cancer. *See* Breast cancer; Cervical cancer
Career choice, 207, 239, 252, 256, 257, 268, 573
Career development, 175
Cervical cancer, 398, 400
Child care, 185, 205, 295, 297, 315, 316, 318, 324, 325, 328, 340, 364, 412, 541, 571, 572, 594, 595, 609
Child labour, 303
Child rearing, 208, 286, 290, 291, 307, 317, 612
Church projects, 172
Church work, 428, 570, 574
Cliff, Michelle, 56
Collective biography, 102, 103, 125
Colonial policy, 427, 431
Colour, 586
Common Entrance Examinations, 253
Consciousness-raising, 35, 36, 39, 61, 76, 375, 394, 401

See also Sistren Theatre Collective
Continuing education. *See* Adult education
Contraception, 208, 269, 276, 277, 278, 279, 281, 282, 283, 285, 286, 287, 288, 291, 292, 294, 301, 306, 308, 309, 314, 322, 324, 325, 326, 327, 328, 329, 330, 331, 334, 335, 336, 337, 341, 345, 346, 347, 352, 353, 354, 355, 356, 357, 358, 359
Cooper, Afua, 89
Council for Voluntary Social Service, 80
Craig, Christine, 78
Creativity, 242, 244, 612
Cultural development, 49
Cultural heritage, 4, 43, 273, 285, 330
Cumper, Pat, 76

D'Costa, Jean, 47, 104
Dance hall music, 18, 20, 21, 42, 51
Data entry operators, 141, 204
Day care centres, 571, 572
Death. *See* Mortality
Demography, 311, 313, 341, 589
Dependent benefits, 480
See also Pensions
Depression, 370
Development planning, 129, 132, 138, 147, 161, 199, 200, 214, 535, 536, 569, 591, 609, 614
Development projects, 130, 140, 143, 161, 196, 197, 222, 234
Diabetes, 406
Dialect poetry, 15, 17, 19, 43, 58, 59, 81, 98
Disabled women, 601
Discourse strategy, 72

Non-traditional occupations, 130, 179, 193, 201, 268

Nugent, Maria, 114

Nurses, 139, 224, 225
    See also Student nurses

Nurses and Midwives Act, 480, 512

Nursing, 79, 105, 121, 207, 262, 390, 401
    See also Student nurses

Nutrition, 142, 143, 162, 293, 300, 316, 318, 363, 367, 368, 372, 379, 381, 384, 385, 388, 389, 393, 395, 411, 595

Obesity, 367, 385

Occupational health hazards, 405

Occupational roles 170, 171, 258, 260

Older women, 156, 372, 393, 545, 565, 571, 572, 597, 598

Oral history, 24, 122, 123, 421, 531, 542

Organization of Women for Progress, 531

Painters. *See* Artists

Palmer, Opal Adisa. *See* Adisa Palmer, Opal

Pantomimes, 43

Parenting, 290, 291, 317, 320, 332, 333, 468, 541, 566, 576, 588, 612, 613
    See also Motherhood

Paternity, 467, 482, 489

Payne, Dorothy, 71

Pensions, 96, 511, 514, 515, 598
    See also Dependent benefits

People's National Party, 522, 527, 528

Periodicals, 625-637

Petty traders. *See* Higglering

Philanthropy, 79, 615

Physical appearance, 259, 586

Pinks, Debbie, 93

Plantation society, 114, 430, 440, 442

Poets, 5, 6, 15, 17, 18, 19, 23, 40, 45, 55, 58, 59, 66, 67, 68, 74, 77, 78, 81, 82, 91, 95, 98, 101, 103, 113, 119, 120, 124

Political participation, 85, 97, 106, 522, 523, 524, 525, 528, 530, 531, 573, 606

Political views, 125

Popular culture, 18, 20, 21, 51

Popular music, 2, 18, 20, 21, 51

Population distribution, 589

Potters, 94

Pregnant women, 272, 363, 366, 368, 370, 376, 377, 379, 380, 384, 386, 387, 388, 389, 391, 395, 396, 397, 399, 402, 406, 407, 408, 409, 410, 412, 557

Prince, Nancy, 117

Prisoners, 369, 473

Professionals, 102, 141, 144, 169, 171, 180, 184, 228, 230, 237, 250, 422, 436

Property ownership, 423, 464
    See also Marital property

Prostitution, 422, 602

Psychodrama, 29, 32, 33, 375, 394

Psychosexual behaviour, 275, 362,

Radio programmes, 43, 144

Radio talk shows, 72

Rastafarian women, 316, 548, 549, 578, 604, 607, 616, 617, 618, 643

Reggae music, 2, 18, 21

Religion, 559

Religious sanctions, 352

Reproduction, 206, 208, 269, 270, 274, 280, 281, 282, 286, 288,

Appendix 4
Libraries

Bureau of Women's Affairs
18 Ripon Road   Kingston 5   Jamaica
Telephone: 876-929-7144, 929-7145,
   929-7146

Documentation Centre
Institute of Social and Economic
   Research
University of the West Indies
Mona   Kingston 7   Jamaica
Telephone: 876-927-0233
Fax: 927-2409
E-mail: iserdoc@uwimona.edu.jm

Documentation Centre
Planning Institute of Jamaica
8 Ocean Blvd   Kingston   Jamaica
Telephone: 876-967-3690, 967-3691,
   967-3692
Fax: 927-5035

Faculty of Law Library
University of the West Indies
Cave Hill   Barbados
Telephone: 246-425-1310
Fax: 429-6738

The Library
Ministry of Agriculture
Hope Road   Kingston 6   Jamaica
Telephone: 876-927-3576
Fax: 977-0885

The Library
University of the West Indies
Mona   Kingston 7   Jamaica
Telephone: 876-927-2123
Fax: 927-1926
E-mail: library@uwimona.edu.jm

The Library
Urban Development Corporation
12 Ocean Blvd   Kingston   Jamaica
Telephone: 876-922-8507
Fax: 922-9326

National Library of Jamaica
12 East Street
PO Box 823   Kingston   Jamaica
Telephone: 876-922-0620
Fax: 922-5567

Sistren Theatre Collective
20 Kensington Cresent
Kingston 5   Jamaica
Telephone: 876-929-2457

www.ingramcontent.com/pod-product-compliance
Lightning Source LLC
Chambersburg PA
CBHW061748270326
41928CB00011B/2421